PRAISE FOR *THE NEXT ROOM*

"The extraordinary relationship between Jane and her mom Betty yields treasure for us all. This book is a warm hug + a blueprint for awakening all in one! Whether you are grieving the loss of a loved one or simply curious about what happens after death, *The Next Room* is a tender glimpse into the infinite possibilities that love has in store for us."

— Sarah Bamford Seidelmann,
author of *Swimming with Elephants*

"*The Next Room* is an intimate conversation of a story that blends the three-dimensional, spiritual realm into the forefront of our earthly consciousness. It is playful and approachable, yet the seriousness of the content is digestible. Jane Asher packages a narrative of emotion and irony into layered vignettes, windows really, through which the reader looks, sees and experiences relationships. In no time, you find yourself halfway through the book wondering where the time went, a sign of good writing and great reading."

— Teri Citterman, Executive Coach and
author of *From the CEO's Perspective*

"Grief. When you hear the word or see it in print, it takes you to a place. For me, it's never a happy place. I immediately feel pain and my energy is lowered. Jane has found a way to give grief a whole new meaning. It's love. It's honor. It's connection. It's hope. Thank you Jane and thank you Betty for opening your hearts to us. I look forward to having more Betty in my life."

— Terry Jaymes. Host of the nationally syndicated
radio show. *Lex and Terry*. Host of the Gang of Two
ıs) the Terry Jaymes Alive podcast.

"I guess I was expecting a nice family story, with Midwest roots, about a daughter's deep and loving relationship with her mother. I didn't know it would turn into a conversation with God! I was ecstatically surprised. I love everything about Jane Asher's first book.

I'd possibly raise an eyebrow if the revelations and wisdom shared by Jane's mother and her tribe from the other side weren't so completely in sync and confirming with everything we've been shown by our 24-year-old son who was tragically killed in an accident in 2008. Jane Asher and her mother who transitioned in 2010 bring down the veil and give us an amazing and wonderful glimpse of what's next after this life.

Jane asks all the questions I kick myself for not asking during our many sessions with mediums. 'Who is God?' 'What is the purpose of this life?' 'Is reincarnation real?' 'What's it like after we shed our bodies?' 'Where do you go?' 'What do you do?' 'Does God love people who do bad things?' 'Do we remain connected with our loved ones who have transitioned?' 'How do we do that?'

During one of their conversations, Jane's mother cautions 'Our book will not be for everyone…It's for you and me and anyone else who cares to join us on this miraculous journey.'

If you're even a little bit curious about the afterlife and what's 'next,' then climb on board, cinch your seatbelt tight, and get ready for just maybe the ride of your life in *The Next Room*."

— Casey Gauntt, **author of** *Suffering is the Only Honest Work* **and** *When the Veil Comes Down*

"*The Next Room* is a story of neverending love. Jane shares her touching story from grief to connection and communication. It's an important book for everyone, and goes far beyond her personal journey. There are messages of love for all of humanity from the Next Room."

— **Brent Carey, Owner of Empower Radio Network**

"Who co-writes a life-changing book with her mother? Then we discover that although Jane's writing partner has "left the room," Mom has "leveled-up" and still has much to share, not only with her daughter but all of us baffled by life or suffering a loss. Love "The Box" philosophy! This book evolves from personal love and loss to expansive awakening."

— **Judy McNutt, The Writer's Gift Mentor**

"I began reading *The Next Room* when darkness was clouding my heart and each word brought in more light. Whether or not you believe in the next room (or life after death), Jane allows you first to become a part of her loving family and then to travel with her through death and grief to connection, self-acceptance and love. Using her own wisdom and the love and guidance of her beloved mother, she answers unanswerable questions in a way that touches heart, mind and soul. I can't tell you where reading *The Next Room* will lead you, but I'm a rather skeptical person and it filled me with comfort and hope."

— **Jan Warner,** *Grief Day by Day: Daily Guidance and Simple Practices for Living with Loss*; Facebook.com/GriefSpeaksOut

THE NEXT ROOM

JANE ASHER
with Betty Asher

CONTENTS

PART THREE – ME, MOM & PAM

PART FOUR – CONVERSATIONS WITH MOM

FOREWORD

It's rare to see a mother and daughter graciously cooperate to pen a book together. But to discover that they wrote this book together from different sides of "the veil" is even more astounding!

This wonderful true story is a not only a testament to the enduring power of love, it's also an inspirational account of how love and life transcend death.

For those of you who have lost loved ones, and for those of you who are interested in what happens after we cross over, this book is very enlightening, authentic, encouraging, and comforting. The wisdom and guidance that is shared from the other side is invaluable.

Jane and her mother Betty share an extraordinarily special bond, in this world and beyond. This story proves that people always remain connected through love and throughout time.

During the process of connecting with Betty in her new realm, I was moved to see how dedicated she was to her daughter and her family. She wasn't contacting Jane because she was stuck and couldn't let go of her earthly life; Betty was choosing to continue to connect with her family, to comfort and guide them. The compassionate Betty, hoping to help her family not grieve so deeply, wanted them all to know that she was happy and surrounded by many loving Beings. In addition, she was eager to share what she was seeing and experiencing in the special realm she had just entered. It was Betty who encouraged Jane to write this book so that together they could share the insights and wisdom that Betty was discovering in her new life.

Many of you may have experienced inconsolable grief when you lost a loved one. Hopefully the amazing descriptions and explanations Betty shares here will offer you enduring reassurance, comfort, and inner peace.

The beautiful approach that Jane takes in this story is truly touching and heart-opening. She brings you intimately into her family life so that you can fully experience the entire process. She shares her genuine thoughts and feelings, which hopefully will validate any feelings you've had during your losses as well.

What Betty shares with Jane about the other side ("The Next Room") is exciting and revealing. There are also some surprises, even for me! And I've been talking with others on the other side of the veil for decades. Betty offers high level teachings and soul guidance. She discusses so many great topics: why we're here on the planet, where humanity is headed, the meaning of the times we're in now, insights that can help us on our life journey, the mistaken beliefs many have held about the afterlife, and more.

It's inspiring to see someone in another dimension so committed to sharing this profound knowledge with those here who may be wondering what happens when we cross over. Jane and Betty are dedicated to bringing this positive and illuminating information to everyone. Please know this — you will see your treasured loved ones again!

There will be no fear of death once people realize there actually is no death, that our souls continue and that there are many Beings helping us from the other side. This true story is a genuine gift to humanity.

— Pamala Oslie, author of *Life Colors, Love Colors, Make Your Dreams Come True,* and *Infinite You*

PROLOGUE

The person with whom I have felt an indelible bond with my whole life died when I was 49 years old. She was, or should I say, still is—my mom, Betty Asher.

Shortly after she passed away, I started having vivid visitations from her while sleeping. These exchanges were deep and unbounded, much different from a regular dream. I felt an uncanny link to her, and each time these communications carried with them significant messages. Right around the same time, she began leaving my family and me dimes. Then, after a spellbinding manifestation through the eyes of her best friend, I knew that Mom was urging me to pay attention. I began recording everything as it was happening. My fascination to write about this ever-growing mystical connection became a passion that I could no longer deny.

I hear a voice deep inside me where only my knowing is found. This intuition seems to be singing a sweet song that only I can hear, although I can't quite make out all the words or notes. They come in flashes. It's as though an invisible muse is breathing oxygen into this book and beckoning me to come along for the ride.

Over the years since Mom disappeared from my sight, our story continued to evolve and unfold. It would overrun me many times, like a puzzle with endless pieces scattered across 10 years of memories, two laptops, and numerous journals. Baffled but driven, I started to collect these fragments and gradually put them together.

The suggestion to involve my friend, Pam Oslie, was initially inspired by my big sister, Lynn. Pam is a well-known psychic medium with the ability to connect with the other side. She had been an unexpected comfort to my father just after my mom died.

The epiphany to involve Pam occurred while I was on a plane writing a letter to Lynn. I was deeply distraught and weighed down with a carry-on bag packed full of heartache and grief. The only thing that brings me solace when I'm in this state is writing. So, I took out a pen and wrote on the only piece of paper I could find—my boarding pass.

The question I posed to my sister through this letter was, "How do I ask our mother to co-author this book with me?"

Clarification seemed to materialize out of thin air. I heard my straight-forward, no-nonsense sister's voice in my head, suggesting that I ask my friend Pam to assist in connecting me with mom to write our story—together.

I immediately sensed my big sister beside me and knew she was doing what she had always done for me my entire life. She was once again giving me stable direction and advice. Lynn never had to make a lot of noise to get her point across. She could do so flawlessly with the tilt of her head, flare of her nostrils, or a flash of her intelligent green eyes. The flight that I was on when this lightning bolt of communication occurred with my sister was my return trip home after *her funeral*.

So, how exactly does one receive messages of divine guidance from their mother when she is no longer in this realm, but in The Next Room? Mom says, "With faith." And so, our story begins, with me, my mom, my psychic friend, and a fortuitous nudge from my big sister Lynn—who had just been buried. With a sizable leap of limitless faith and my puppy at my feet, I open up to receive and write.

But first—the letter.

DEAR LYNN

Sunday, April 10th, 2016 – At an altitude of 38,000 feet, en route to San Diego from Detroit.

Dear Lynn,

I realize that I recently saw you before this final trip home and that would've been the time to ask for your advice. Because of the circumstances surrounding our last visit, I didn't have the heart and it seemed you were lacking the strength to form the words. I also didn't feel it was fair to bother you, especially since you *lie dying*.

Throughout my life, I've always valued your opinion, as you well know. I have turned to you over and over again in times of confusion. You have always listened, before offering your ideas on whatever the matter would be. Since you are no longer physically here, this letter will have to do—for now, anyway.

Thank you for not laughing in my face when I told you a while back that I was thinking of writing a book. My entire life I have fantasized about the notion. I have only shared that idea with a handful of people—you and our niece, Carey. Carey was pivotal in supporting the initial idea I was kicking around. I remember the exact moment that our conversation took place. I was in the folks' front yard picking up sticks and branches that had blown off the big oak trees and I was trying to get a handle on my emotions and calm myself (miserably, I might add). I was agitated, an emotional mess, and, at the peak of my frustration, my cell phone rang. It seems as though Carey has an uncanny knack of sensing when I need to vent the most. I suppose that's why Tom nicknamed her Yoda. In great detail, I shared with Carey why I was so upset, while continuing to pick up the sticks in the front yard. Carey listened to me go on and on and then she stopped me and said, "Aunt Jane, I think this is your book—you need to write about this."

In the very instant that Carey uttered those words, I had a full body rush—you know, the kind that travels from the hair on top of your head to the tips of your toes? This feeling is what Pastor Rick used to lovingly refer to as "the Holy Spirit tingle." I distinctly recall sensing at that moment in time that I was receiving a divine message. The delivery method just happened to be through the voice of our wise little niece, Yoda.

Okay, Lynn, so here's my confusion and questions that seem to be surrounding me around this crazy idea—

Will Mom agree to write this with me? And how on Earth do I write a book with Mom, while I'm on this side and she is in The Next Room? Also, where do I start? And finally, how exactly do I do this, as I do not know how to even write a book? All of this unwelcomed turbulence seems to be taking a spin on the hamster wheel in my head.

Whoa. It's so wild, Lynn, but I literally just felt you burst into my thoughts at the very moment I started wondering how I was going to ask mom if she would write this with me.

Even though you've only been gone a week, I feel your strong presence and energy swirling around me. I sense your guidance on a deep level and I distinctly hear your voice right now. And, if I'm picking up clearly on what I'm hearing, you are suggesting that I ask my friend Pam if she'd be willing to help me, by connecting with Mom.

Holy shit, Lynn! I absolutely love the idea of involving Pam. Thank you so much for the notion. Pam has an undeniable gift of being able to communicate clearly with the other side.

What amazes me is that you and I are physically so far apart, but I feel you here with me right now. I'll reach out to Pam as soon as this plane lands and ask her if she's willing to see if Mom is open and available to write this book with me.

Well, as usual, Lynn, you helped me work through an issue I'm having, simply by listening. Damn, I miss you so much my teeth even ache. You have been my go-to sounding board for years. I sure hope you know how much I love and appreciate you. I seriously don't know how I'm going to figure all of this out without you physically here by my side.

I hear you again, espousing your favorite lines, "Pull up your big girl panties, Jane, and get on with it." After all, "It is what it is." Right?

I'll write again soon, and I'll let you know if Mom agrees to write this book with me.

Ha! Who am I kidding? As close as you and Mom are right now, you'll be the first to know!

I love you more.

Your baby sister, Jane

Dear Lynn Marie, ~~I have I just say~~ Sunday, April 3rd, 2016 ~~(somewhere over the United States on the plane)~~

I have been thinking about writing this book for five years and six months. The idea honestly was inspired by our niece Carey when I was picking up sticks in the folks front yard in Oxford. I was really upset that day. Carey called me right at the peak of my frustration — As she happens to do (Carey always has this uncanny way of sensing when I need her most). I suppose that is why my husband nicknamed her Yoda. Anyway — I told Carey what was bothering me in great detail — And she said "Aunt Jne, I think this is your book — you need to write about this." — I can't tell you how the goose bumps/body rush hit me from the top of my head to the tip of my toes ~~at that exact moment~~. I only had one big problem... Would she write it with me? Here's the tricky part — I wasn't sure she would say yes. I desperately needed, wanted and had to have her say Yes — would she think I was being silly? How do I ask her to be my Co-Author — And... what if she turned her back on me? I know what you're going to say to me without even asking — you're going to say Jne — just go for it. After all. It is what it is. ..."

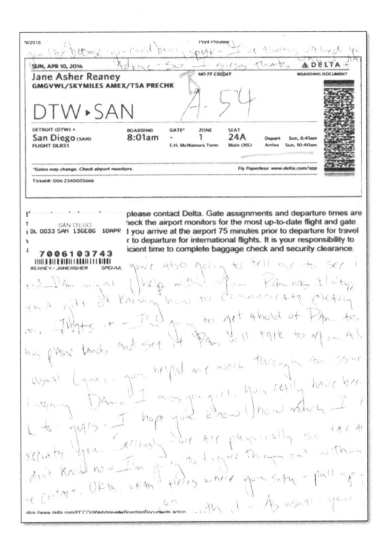

PART ONE
GROWING UP

PART ONE PRAYER

I roll out of bed and gently drop to the floor on my knees. A soft, merciful murmur takes form as words of gratitude tumble forth from a humble space deep inside of me. As a tap of truth arrives, my spirit soars. I open up to receive this peaceful invitation.

I lean in. A deep cleansing breath fills my lungs as I bring my hands to the location where my tender heart resides. I bow my head.

> **Dear Lord, the Almighty Energy of All, please align me with my reason for being. I fearlessly ask for your divine loving light to shine upon me. Fill me with your Holy Spirit, and guide this story forth with integrity, truth and grace.**
>
> **In your name I pray,**
>
> **Amen.**

CHAPTER ONE

Magnetic Mom

Everyone who met her, loved her. She was extremely easy to look at. Her eyes were the color of a clear blue sky on a cloudless spring day. Her smile was a little crooked and set off to the left, certainly a Harmon trait. It welcomed you deep into her world. Her smile was not only available for loved ones and friends, but for complete strangers, too.

You were not a stranger for long once you met her. She had the magical gift of drawing you in with little effort whatsoever. She was like a powerful magnet in a room full of flimsy dollar store paper clips. Everyone seemed to be comforted in her presence and immediately felt a willingness wash over them to share with her the darkest corners of their thoughts or bewildered feelings. It was as though you *needed* her to listen to you.

Often, people would walk up to her on the beach, at a restaurant, or at a cocktail party just to be near her. When someone would ask for her advice, she would always ask, "Do you really want to hear what I have to say?" If your response was, "Yes," you'd better brace yourself. She was never mean spirited with her words, just honest and direct. To use an old boxing phrase, she never pulled a punch. She hit you straight between the eyes with every ounce of her generous intuition.

I honestly don't know from where the wisdom bubbled up. It seemed to come from somewhere deep inside of her. It was almost as if the secrets of the universe were embedded in her belly and you felt as though she was put here on Earth to help guide you gently along on your journey.

CHAPTER TWO

The Angel Box

It sat untouched for eight years, hidden from sunlight and human contact. I slowly reach for my pain. It comes in the form of an angel box—a small treasure chest with purple and gold angels, the words *peace* and *joy* adorning inside and out.

Looks are deceiving. There are no sparkling riches inside. It is filled with desolate sorrow that I submerged and stuffed down in the dark recesses of my memory, years ago. The top of the angel box is dusty from sitting for years on the bottom of my closet behind my shoes. I wipe it off with a well-worn rag. I sit down in my reading chair with the angel box resting on my lap. I inhale deeply and slowly exhale. As I open the lid, the realization hits me that the contents are waiting to throw 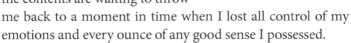 me back to a moment in time when I lost all control of my emotions and every ounce of any good sense I possessed.

I smell old paper and ink mixed with my now-dried tears. It's an assault on my senses. I sift through the over-flowing box of notes, letters, and old journals, knowing this

nearly weightless pile of memories has the capacity to physically and spiritually crush me. All of these painful moments
had been recorded long ago and stored away for another day.
I tentatively reach for the small pink notebook that I know
contains a tormenting, bone-crushing ache.

I stop quickly. A harsh slap of shame stings my cheek.
I'm not ready.

The dance continues. My heart begs to stay on the outer
edges of this suffering, far away from the recognition of my
deep despondency. I shut the lid. The courage I crave to
revisit my tortured words is missing. This distressing chapter
will have to wait for another day, when I am strong enough
to handle the pain that is contained inside the angel box.

CHAPTER THREE

My Little Pink Notebook

My beautiful mother was born with a heart murmur that worsened as she aged. By the time she was in her early 80s, her doctor recommended seeing a cardiologist, which she did. The heart doctor explained that the valve was getting smaller and what should have been the size of a dime was now about the size of the head of a straight pin. This resulted in a massive reduction in oxygen, which left her tired and many times struggling to breathe. That's a hard thing to deal with when you are a woman who is always on the go. My running joke about my mom is that she could simultaneously prepare a meal and burp a baby while fixing the perfect Bloody Mary, all with one hand tied behind her back. Quite simply, she was a superhero of a woman.

With her situation getting worse by the day, she had two options: she could have heart valve replacement surgery or risk a sudden massive heart attack that could result in her immediate death. After consultation with my dad, each of us children, and her beloved general practitioner, the decision was made to move forward with the operation. Her surgery was scheduled for mid-August. I made a resolution after speaking with my husband, my siblings, and my dad, that

I would be on the "Bring Mom Home from the Hospital" committee. I was looking forward to pampering her by rubbing her back, brushing her hair and cooking her healthy meals. I booked a flight to arrive approximately a week after her surgery, which by all indications seemed ample time to get her back up on her feet and home.

I was told she came through the surgery with flying colors. I could not wait to kiss her sweet face. I was disappointed to find that she was still in the hospital when I arrived. She wasn't gaining her strength as quickly as the doctors would have liked. My dad and I visited her every day. She was in decent spirits, but something just wasn't right. Four days after I arrived, Dad and I went to the hospital for our daily visit. When we walked into her room, we could immediately sense that something was wrong. Mom was flush and she wasn't speaking. I told Dad to sit in the chair by her bed and keep talking to her while I ran to get help. The minute the staff entered her room, a flurry of activity began, as they knew she needed to be transferred back to the ICU. They wheeled her out of her room so quickly that they banged her bed into the door frame on the way out. She looked up at me with absolute terror in her eyes. It was one of those moments that you wish you could erase from your memory.

The look in her eyes haunts me to this day. I mumbled something like, "You'll be okay. I love you," as they wheeled her out of sight. I walked back to her room to get my dad. He was just sitting in her now-empty room with a look of total bewilderment etched on his troubled face. I held out my hand and said, "Come on, Dad. Let's go back to the waiting room. It's more comfortable there." He followed me like a dutiful little boy. It was surreal moment. As I walked him down the hospital corridor, it felt as if I was leading him toward a landslide of ruin and pain. Once in the waiting room, I placed a Bible in his hands and said, "Here, you read this while I go see what's going on." It didn't take long. Her medical team was actually on their way to find us. The doctor and a nurse asked to speak with us in private. Dad just nodded at me, as if to say, "You go." Looking back, I know now he was in shock. They escorted me to an empty room and said, "We need to open her back up. *It's her only chance.*" They shoved a clipboard full of papers in front of me to sign, which I quickly did. The transaction took less than thirty seconds, but it is forever branded in slow motion in my mind's eye.

Even as I sit here and write about this now, I feel like a vice is squeezing my rib cage and a golf ball-size lump has taken up residence in my throat. This agonizing memory is fused with enough potent power that even after 10 years it yields the strength to physically wreck me. Being the youngest of the family, I never ever fathomed that I would have to deal with the emotional duress that comes with making such an imposing decision on my own.

I returned to the waiting room to fill Dad in on what the doctors had just told me. We sat there together in utter silence, completely lost in our individual suffering. The only sound in that small waiting room that day was our collective hearts beating as loudly as the sound of a high school drum team. I excused myself and stepped out in the hall to begin the process of informing all of my siblings of our mother's dire situation.

Oldest to youngest, I called Lynn first. She was already up to her ass in alligators after her husband, Cal, was literally run over by a car two weeks earlier. The minute I heard her voice, I started to cry. Lynn insisted that I remain strong, especially for Dad. So, in essence, "Buck up, little sister." Gail was next. She immediately started making arrangements to hop in her car and head north. On to Patti—she and her husband Burt made a plan to come as soon as possible. To add to their complications, Burt's mother was in hospice at the time. Donna, who lived locally, drove over to the hospital immediately after we hung up the phone. And lastly, my brother Tom, who happened to already be on his way to visit Mom when my emergency call reached him. With my bases covered, I went back in the waiting room to sit, pray, and hold my big daddy's hand, while we waited for the reinforcement of my siblings to arrive.

Dad, Donna, Tom, and I all waited anxiously for any news. It was many hours later before we heard anything from the team of doctors who had taken Mom down to the emergency operating room. When they finally came to speak with us, they were brief. All they said to us was, "She's alive and on life support in the ICU." Depleted and numb, we took the unusually paltry token of her being alive as a win. We went home to try and rest.

I knew I had to do something. Besides praying, writing was the only thing I could think to do. Writing centers me. I have volumes of gratitude journals, notebooks packed with dreams, numerous notes on my phone, and even have some random scraps of paper stuck in books with little pieces of stories I have hopes of writing someday. When Mom had to be opened up again, my first thought was that I need to write all of this down. In the bottom of my backpack, I found a small pink spiral notebook that said "Notes" on the front. I carried that little notebook to and from the hospital every day. In my *crazy, wild-eyed, my-mom's-not going-to-die* mode, I hounded the doctors, asking questions. I stalked them, lurking in the shadows to eavesdrop on their conversations, all the while writing everything down in my small pink notebook. I made no attempt to keep track of my notes in any orderly fashion. I just wrote. I wish now I would have been more organized. The pages are a raging mess, much like the emotions I was experiencing the entire time my mother was fighting for her life in the ICU.

The following day, the surgeon that had performed her emergency surgery, along with an infectious disease expert, agreed to sit down with all of us in a conference room—Dad, Gail, Patti, Donna, Tom, and me, with Lynn on speaker from her home. I had my little pink notebook. Mom was alive but gravely ill and on maximum life support. Gravely struck me as a word that no one should ever have to hear about a loved one's condition.

She had contracted an infection, which had attacked her new heart valve. She had a central PICC line going into her chest, as meds could not pass through her veins because the tissue was so damaged. A machine was assisting her heart to beat with a balloon that was inserted through her groin. A ventilator pumped oxygen into lungs. The doctor said he hoped there wasn't any liver damage but was not very reassuring. She was hooked up to everything but the kitchen sink, just to keep her alive. My mother was explicit in her wishes and had a DNR firmly in place. She often said to us, "If any of you children try to keep me alive by having me hooked up to machines, I will come back and haunt you." Although we all knew her wishes well, we also knew that this would not be her endgame. This is not how our strong, magnetic, loving, generous mother was leaving the planet. Somehow, the thought of removing the machines and allowing her to die was not even part of the conversation, not even for a murmur of heartbeat.

The day after my brother arrived at my folks' place, Tom, Dad, and I went back to the hospital. We were allowed in her room, but only two at a time. Throughout the day, we took turns sitting with her, praying and expressing our love. My once-vivacious mother in an induced coma and hooked up to machines was the most excruciating scene I had ever witnessed. At the end of another long day of sitting vigil, my brother took my dad home to rest and I stayed behind. Patti and her husband were about to arrive at the hospital. I told Dad I would catch a ride home with them. What Dad didn't know was that I had no intention of leaving my mother. Now that I had someone staying and keeping Dad company at the house, I could stay close to Mom.

Across the street from the hospital was an inexpensive place to stay that was affiliated with the hospital. It was extremely sparse. The stairs led down to rooms that were underground and surrounded by brick walls. It was the perfect place to thrash, wail, curse, and scream at the top of my lungs—my very own little bunker of pain. I was pissed off at God, but after pleading, crying, demanding, and begging with the big guy, I found no peace. I don't think God was listening to me anyway. I detest being yelled at, so I'm assuming God didn't dig it either. I decided I had to see Mom again.

I walked back across the street, snuck in the emergency entrance, and cautiously wound my way back up to the ICU. I found Mom in her quiet, dark room. The only sounds were the machines huffing and puffing to keep her alive. The night nurse seemed understanding and allowed me to stay. She didn't want to answer any of my questions as she wearily eyed my pink notebook. I stood at my mother's bedside feeling like a lost little 10-year-old girl. I couldn't speak. I just stood there wordlessly looking down at my hero who was being kept alive artificially with the assistance of modern technology, all while thinking, *"I don't know how I'm going to live without you."*

The entire week Mom was in the ICU, Dad and all six of us children continued to flow in and out of her room. Each of us encouraged her in our own way to get better. It was only two days after my disturbing, yet cathartic, screaming festival at God that something unbelievable occurred. My mom's numbers started to head in the desired direction. With each passing moment, we tacitly celebrated her tenacity and determination. It was a miracle—the kind you only read about or see in the movies. My mother was defying the cosmic force to pull her from this earthly plane. As one machine after another was removed, she showed each of us her astonishing desire and determination to not have her final chapter written from the hospital—*in my little pink notebook.*

CHAPTER FOUR

Invisible Shroud

One by one, the machines were removed, and finally Mom was able to communicate. Every day, as we had been camping out in the hospital to be near her, Dad had regaled me with (his side) of their love story. I teasingly asked her if she chased after him when they were courting, as he claimed. She smiled and said, "Evidently." I knew in that moment that my witty and aware mother was returning to life and on her way to a full recovery!

Gail is my second-oldest sister. She and I were together when we got the best news. Mom was getting stronger by the minute and they wanted to move her out of the ICU and into a regular room, possibly as soon as the following day. It was music to our ears. Gail and I were so elated that we started belting out an extremely vigorous version of *Let Your Smile Be Your Umbrella* while in the hospital ladies' room. The acoustics kicked ass—far better than you would expect for a hospital bathroom. We made several women laugh that day.

It was Labor Day when Mom was moved out of the ICU. She was weak but anxious to get the feeding tube out so she could have real food. A few days later, she was finally strong enough to graduate from her hospital room to the on-site rehabilitation center. Dad and I arrived early that morning. I helped Mom with her shower. It was an extreme amount of exertion for a woman who was on maximum life support just a few days earlier, but she handled it with conviction and grace.

I had by then been by my mom's side for eighteen days in a row. We both knew I needed to get back home. It took several minutes that morning for us to discuss the distressing prospect of me leaving. Not only had I been off work the entire time, but my son, Thomas, would be having his 14th birthday in just a few days and she did not want me to miss that. Classic mom, here she is in major full recovery mode, still thinking of others. I assured her that I would catch a flight and be home in time to celebrate my son's birthday. She told me where his gift from her was back at the house and asked if I would wrap it for her. Who thinks about other people's needs when they are in the hospital? My mother does, of course. Since neither of us wanted to say goodbye, we discussed a little more about her move to the rehabilitation wing of the hospital and of the next time we would be together. We both thought it would, no doubt, be in her cozy home, having a visit over morning coffee or an afternoon cocktail.

Even though it agonized me to leave her side, we both knew I needed to return home to my life and family in San Diego. I also knew she had the all-encompassing support of my siblings, nieces, nephews, and, of course, my dad. I kissed her on the forehead and told her I loved her. What I didn't realize at the time was that it would be last tender moment I would ever share with my extraordinary mother. I flew home wearing an invisible shroud of hesitation.

CHAPTER FIVE

COMING HOME

I reluctantly returned to my day-to-day life in San Diego while my mom was busting her butt in the hospital rehabilitation center so she could go home. She did every single thing they asked of her. She pushed, pulled, and prodded her body forward. She willed herself to regain the strength she needed to finally make it back to her beloved home with the love of her life, my dad. I was 2,400 miles away but felt like I was right by her side the entire time. Each morning, I rolled out of bed and dropped to my knees, not so much to pray, but to beg God to allow her to get stronger and be able to go home. Even though I had recently yelled hysterically and had a hissy fit directed at God I was banking on the forgiveness that I've read about in several Bible verses. I was hopeful the absolution thing rang true, and that God didn't hold a grudge. Meanwhile, my dad, my four sisters, my brother, in-laws, a few grandchildren, and a couple of close friends rotated in to visit Mom while she was unfaltering in her efforts to get the hell out of that facility.

In mid-September, after 13 days of dogged determination, she was finally well enough to be checked out of the rehab center. Donna—the fourth-oldest—and Dad were there to pick Mom up and bring her home. Hearing this news long distance made my heart swell, just like that scene from the Grinch.

Three days after Mom came home, Lynn went to see her. I called to check up on Mom and Lynn told me that Mom wanted to invite their best friends, Bob and Ruthie Schlang, over for cocktails. I questioned Mom about having this gathering, wondering if she was up for it. She assured me that she not only wanted to do this, but it was her idea. It was yet another example of her dynamic persistence. Even though she had just returned from a harrowing 36-day hospital ordeal, she wanted to be with her daughter, my dad, and their best friends in a celebratory fashion.

As usual and in perfect Lynn style, she took care of all the details. She prepared hors d'oeuvres and mixed drinks, and helped fulfill yet another of my mother's wishes. What no one realized at the time was that this celebration would be one of her final wishes because just five days later she was gone.

CHAPTER SIX

SEPTEMBER 31

My mother slipped from the arms of her best friend (my dad) and into The Next Room on a Friday. It was September 31, 2010.

Wait, what? To my knowledge and I'm sure yours, thirty days hath September, right?

Not in 2010, at least according to the calendar that hung on the back of my kitchen door. My mother had given me that calendar, as she had done each and every year since I was a young woman, when I moved from Michigan to California. It was packed full of her little handwritten notes on the little boxes of each date to remind me of family birthdays, anniversaries, and other important events, with an occasional smiley face for good measure.

I chuckle to myself, thinking back to the Christmas when she sent just the calendar, sans notes. I packed it in my suitcase, and, when I flew home that following summer, insisted she sit in her glider rocking chair and fill out that calendar as she did every other year. She called me a *little shit* and we laughed as she filled out my calendar, flipping through hers as reference.

This small but thoughtful gift was her way of sharing the things she held most meaningful about our big, boisterous family. And of course, it was a not-so-subtle reminder that I should send a card or make a phone call to these family members on their special day. Since I was the first and only one to move out of Michigan all those years ago, she did not want me to lose my close connection to the family.

In 2010, neither my husband, my children, nor I initially noticed that our calendar that year had included an additional day in September.

In my grief-stricken autopilot, I went to work immediately, planning our trip home. Even though my husband begged me to stop and experience my grief, I could not. I had to get home. I had to be by my father's side. I grabbed the calendar from the back of the kitchen door and started calling the airlines. As I was flipping between September and October, I noticed the extra day. *Friday, September 31.*

SEPTEMBER 2010

SUN	MON	TUE	WED	THU	FRI	SAT
			1	2	3	4
5	6 *Labor Day*	7	8	9	10	11 *Thomas 14*
12	13 *Nana's B'day*	14	15 *Big Bill B'day*	16	17 *Pat B'day*	18 *Marcie B'day*
19	20	21	22	23	24	25 *James & Tom anniversary 77 y*
26	27	28	29 *Bridget B'day*	30	31	

That day is wedged in my memory along with the traumatic sensation of how that long-distance call from Michigan made me feel. I will never forget the words that Lynn spoke in measured anguish that day. "Janey, she's gone. Mom died." Those five small words shot a searing white-hot dagger of visceral pain through my entire body and made me cave forward as a guttural sound of torment tore through me. It was a sound I had surely never made before, nor have I repeated since.

After the call, all that was left in the place where my beating heart would normally dwell was a pitted space filled with abject misery. The loss was so monumental that, even now, it has the ability to randomly overwhelm my senses. It is a dull throbbing that visits, unannounced, like an uninvited guest at a dinner party. Its influence is so commanding that it often brings me to tears in the middle of my morning walk, driving my car, or simply observing hummingbirds in my backyard. It is a tidal wave of misery that rolls over me without asking permission, leaving in its wake a dismal residue like random litter on a pristine beach. These bitter pangs of pain are recurring reminders that my mother—my mentor, my rock and guiding light—is gone. She carried me for nine months and uplifted me for 49 years. So, it makes perfect sense to me now why time was suspended and the imaginary date of her death was created. As my husband pointed out, she didn't really die. She merely slipped into The Next Room on a day that doesn't really exist. It's curious to me, but somehow it makes everything just a little bit softer, knowing that a new day was created in this time space continuum for her to transition.

As the day approaches each year, a day that normally does not appear on a calendar has become a wordless reminder that my spirited, influential, strong mother has never really left. She may have vanished from sight on September 31, 2010, but I know with every fiber of my being that she is still here with me now. It's been almost 11 years since she transitioned. I feel the undeniable urge to start piecing together the jigsaw puzzle of potent memories, old journal entries, social media posts, and her seasoned hand-written letters, and finally gather it all under one roof—our book.

From her transcendent vantage point, Mom is sharing her perspective on forgiveness, grace, gratitude, kindness, compassion, love, and the Almighty Energy of All—God. These fascinating morsels of her truth are tumbling forth. She is reaching out and I am listening. My mother is my co-author. This is *her* story, *my* story, *our* story from here and beyond, in a day out of time from The Next Room.

CHAPTER SEVEN

DAD'S REALIZATION

It was only a couple of days after my mother departed from her living room into The Next Room that my entire immediate family started to roll into the northern Michigan town of Gaylord, which would be her final resting place. All of the love, laughter, home-cooked meals, card games, and deep conversations that once took place were now just a deluge of memories tucked away until the pain subsided. Little did I know that the distress would be forever present. It never leaves. It just morphs and changes shape and form over time, sometimes pretending to hide—much like a kid playing hide-and-seek but not quite getting the hiding part, their little ass hanging out from behind the couch.

The house is a solid, cozy place, just a quick 45-minute drive down from the Mackinaw Bridge, which famously links Michigan's lower and upper peninsulas. Gaylord's downtown is referred to as the Alpenstrasse, which is also a famous route in Germany. The architecture replicates a German village. It's a safe and quaint town. My parents had a marvelous piece of land about three miles from downtown on the right-hand side of Buck Road, which dead-ends in front of their horseshoe-shaped driveway. Just across the road is Lake Otsego, which is a six-mile-long, super-clean freshwater lake. It's perfect for water skiing and boating in the summer and snowmobiling and ice fishing in the winter. The house was set approximately 100 yards from the lake and the property was artfully landscaped with huge oak trees. My mother always said it reminded her of a little park. It was very much her own little park.

My dad and his extremely colorful younger brother, Doug, built the place before they moved from their big house across the street. I have vivid memories of my Uncle Doug. He drove a Harley Davidson, had a membership at the local Moose Lodge, drank scotch on the rocks, and had a throaty baritone laugh that would bring a smile to even the toughest curmudgeon. His smell was comforting—a manly blend of wood and tobacco. His hugs were legendary. He would squeeze me in a hug so hard, a fart would slip out. He even baked me a homemade German chocolate cake for my 21st birthday. Uncle Doug was the coolest.

My mother loved her home. It was her sanctuary. So, of course, it makes total sense to me that she chose to take her last breath on her treasured turf in the adoring arms of her best friend and husband. There were two bedrooms and an upstairs attic that is only accessible by a trapdoor that pulls down to reveal a hidden folding staircase. It's a secret gem. The house also has a kickass Great Room with a big rock fireplace. The middle stone is heart shaped. Not everyone notices the heart. To me, it's the cornerstone of the entire house and speaks volumes about the energy of their home. Although a great party house, it's only large enough for one family to stay there at a time.

I really can't say how the arrangements for my mom's celebration of life came together. At the time, I was in a hazy state of melancholy and not exactly aware of details. But come together it did. When all of us are together, it's a sizable crew. We rented cabins a mile away for the days leading up to Mom's funeral. It was a full-on Asher commune, with lots of food, cases of cold beer, and a football to toss around as we collectively grieved our agonizing loss.

It was decided before we arrived from San Diego that my family would stay in the house with Dad. I suppose it was because we traveled the farthest. My sisters intuitively knew that it would not be as gloomy and depressing for our children if they stayed with their cousins at the cabins. So, it ended up being just my husband and me staying with Dad.

The morning after we arrived, I woke up early to work on Mom's eulogy. The house was uncommonly quiet. I was alone with a steaming cup of coffee—and a mammoth invisible hole in my heart. My husband, Tom, was still sleeping, and Dad was in his room. I was sitting in Mom's favorite spot in her gliding rocking chair in the living room with her prayer book in my lap when Dad walked into the room. He stood across from me wearing his grief openly etched on his handsome face. His hair was disheveled, standing on end from another restless night of not sleeping.

With my eyes welling, I looked up at him with expectation. He spoke first and said, "I figured it out."

"What?" I asked him.

"When I woke up this morning, I finally had the answer to something that has been bothering me since your mother left."

He always worked through issues while he slept. He called this process *noodling*. I asked again, "What, Dad? What answer? What did you figure out?"

"Well, ever since your mother passed, I've been feeling so strange. I didn't know why, or what was going on, but now, I know."

"What is it? What did you figure out, Dad?" He had an odd but serene look on his face.

"I realized that when your mother died—she took my heart with her."

Bam. It was a direct hit to *my* heart. Dad's simple but profound recognition rendered me speechless. I felt my misery merge with his as our collective tears uncontrollably flowed in tandem.

After his confession, he actually seemed soothed. It was as though a deep understanding and a generous fulfillment of peace had come over him. He had a rather contented look, like he had single-handedly just discovered all the grand mysteries of the universe. Indeed, he had finally noodled out the reason behind his hollow, empty feeling of nothingness while standing in the exact spot where, only days before, his best friend had slipped from his arms and into The Next Room, *taking his heart with her.*

CHAPTER EIGHT

DECKERVILLE

I was born and raised in the Thumb of Michigan, in the village of Deckerville, which is only seven miles from the shores of the extraordinary Lake Huron. A true Michigander would say, a *quick* 10-minute drive. Deckerville has approximately 800 people, 25 churches, 5,000 cows, two bars, and one blinking yellow traffic light at the one intersection in town. Our school held K-12 in one horseshoe-shaped building. Patti is third-oldest of my sisters. She taught at the school for thirty years, along with a high caliber of other teachers and coaches.

Everyone in the area looked out for one another, and they still do. If one person is facing a challenge or is hurting, everyone rises up to help. The support will vary, based on needs of the individual. It may be a fund-raising spaghetti dinner, a golf tournament for charity, or a casserole delivered to your door when someone passes away. There is always an astonishing display of communal generosity. I am eternally grateful that I was wrapped in the arms of this small town's love as I spent the first eighteen years on the planet in Deckerville, and I wouldn't have changed a thing. My mom and dad were married in 1948 and loved each other for 62 years. It wasn't all rainbows and unicorns, but, from my limited perception as the youngest child, it was about as good as a relationship gets.

We were, for the most part, a very happy and somewhat normal family. Since there were six of us kids, many times Mom and Dad referred to us by number in the order of birth, especially when they were introducing us.

My oldest sister Lynn, of course, is #1. She was strong, extremely intelligent, pragmatic, very direct, and an overall force of nature. Lynn was born on my dad's birthday and was fond of saying, "I don't have a birthday, it's Dad's birthday." She was right. My dad really loved his birthday and expected everyone to make a fuss over him. Lynn did not usually take the backseat for anyone, but in this instance, she humored our father.

My compassionate sister Gail was next in line. Her motto: "I'm #2, I try harder." I don't think I know anyone on the planet who does more or cares more for others than Gail. It would make your head spin to hear how many good deeds she does in just one day. She is not looking for accolades or praise, it's just how she rolls. She was an excellent student, played piano beautifully and, to my knowledge, never ever got in trouble.

Patti is #3. She's the joker and a comedian who was extremely popular in high school. She is fun and funny—a rare combination — and loves to laugh. I laugh every single time I am with her in person or on the phone. Patti loves life and in return, it loves her. Everyone should have a life-of-the-party-Patti in their life. She just happens to be brilliant as well.

Donna was the fourth child. She is kind, protective, and loyal. When we were growing up, we were close as she was the closest sister to me in age and looked after me. She would perform *trick-tee-dick-tees*, a game she made up to entertain her little sister. She would lie on her back on the floor while hoisting me in the air with her feet on my tummy so I could simulate flying. This memory still makes me smile. Donna was also athletic and made the varsity cheerleading squad as a high school freshman.

My brother Tom is #5. I scored the big brother—I nick-named him the *Broster*. He has an easy smile and a great sense of humor. His memory is uncanny, and he can do complicated math in his head. He was, and still is, my best buddy. We played red rover, hide-n-seek, and tag with the other neighborhood kids every single night until the streetlights came on. He was my great protector and looked out for me throughout my childhood and high school years.

Then there's me, #6. The baby. I'm not sure why, but growing up I felt I was supposed to do something significant. Not to say I'm special or superior in any sense; rather it was a subtle inner push to do something just beyond my grasp. When I was ten, I fantasized about becoming a famous singer. I used a big towel to simulate long flowing locks of hair as I looked into the big vanity mirror in my folks' closet. My mom's pretty, blue hairbrush became my microphone and I would belt out "At Last" by Etta James. Another fascination was becoming a spy. No doubt this passion flowed directly from my favorite book, *Harriet the Spy*. One day, I even decided to spy on the next-door neighbors, the Deckers. They were a solid family of quality people and the perfect next-door companions as they had 11 kids and a freezer full of ice cream!

Mom and Dad had deep respect for one another. They were a unified front as parents. If you asked Mom if you could go somewhere and she said no, you knew not to even try to ask Dad. They raised us to be respectful and kind, and to look out for one another, even when life got messy. And it did a few times, like when my sister crashed Dad's car, or my brother stayed out all night. Mom and Dad would go into their bedroom and discuss what needed to happen regarding discipline. They were an impenetrable duo. The two of them were never to be tested against each other.

They were ideal parents in my eyes. Dad was a strapping, strong, industrious man and held down two jobs the entire time I was growing up. It seemed that the only time I really saw him was when he came home for dinner every night at six o'clock. Mom was the quintessential stay-at-home mother. She baked, cooked, and cleaned the house. She did the laundry, including ironing our clothes. She attended every single basketball game and never missed a Girl Scouts or PTA meeting. My mother always smelled so sweet, like a fresh baked apple pie. I loved snuggling with her in their big, king-size bed that took up their entire small, downstairs bedroom. My parents were in sync—always aligned with everything under the roof in our big, old house in Deckerville.

CHAPTER NINE

Treasure Island

For as long as I can remember, Mom and Dad headed south to Florida every year just after Christmas. It was important to them to flee Michigan's famously ridiculous winter weather. If you've ever spent a winter in the Midwest, you know how thankless it can be. It's not just the snow and cold, it's the unyielding grey skies that can stretch for an infinitely long time.

Treasure Island is nestled alongside the Gulf of Mexico just south of Tampa. Mom and Dad discovered this little paradise through their friends, Torchie and his southern belle of a wife, Kay. His real name was Charles, but everyone called him Torchie, possibly because of his flaming red hair. He was a gentleman and extremely accomplished. Aside from being a pilot and boat captain, Torchie was a musician and played the standup bass, which he did often in our family room. It's one of the reasons Big Band music was woven into my spirit at such a tender age.

Treasure Island smelled like what I imagine paradise must smell like—coconut oil and top-shelf tequila. The light is wild and seems to radiate a healing energy that bounces directly off the stunning aqua-blue water and into your soul. The powdery sand on the beach is silky and white and stretches for miles. Its natural beauty beckons for a long amble with no destination in mind. Besides their home, Treasure Island was clearly my folks' other "happy place." It makes perfect sense for them to have fallen head over heels in love, where their old friend Torchie had taken them many moons ago.

My parents initially stayed in Florida just a week or two, but it expanded into a full month by the time I was in high school. By then I was the only kid left under the roof in Deckerville. I was on my own and loved it. I was a teenager with a car, a gas pump in the back yard, and blank checks for groceries. My mother was so thoughtful she even left blank notes in a kitchen drawer with *Thank you, Betty Asher* hand-written at the bottom. These little notes were "just in case of an emergency"—you know, for things like running late for school or skipping out of the first few hours. I had the "emergency" of sleeping in on a regular basis. What made my situation even better is that my folks were friends with the principal and the superintendent of the school. Everyone sort of looked the other way while I had a month-long vacation of my own. My sisters, Lynn, Gail, and Donna were also checking in on me, so I really wasn't left home alone to throw elaborate keggers.

After I graduated high school and left for college, Mom and Dad sold our Deckerville home and moved north to their retirement home in Gaylord. It was right about the time when they began staying the entire winter on Treasure Island.

CHAPTER TEN

THE PLAN

Growing up, Lynn was like a second mother to me. She was calm, logical, and realistic. She didn't get too fired up or flustered over things that would normally stress out the average person. I was only nine when she married Cal and moved out of our childhood home. We were extremely close, but with an age difference of twelve years our true friendship didn't develop until after I was married and had children of my own. As adults, we had a standing Friday night date to talk over the phone. We lovingly referred to that time as *Wine Thirty*. She would open a bottle of wine at her home in Lexington, Michigan, and I would do the same in San Diego. She would jokingly say we were "solving the world's problems."

Several weeks after Mom had passed away, Lynn called and said, "We've got to get Dad out of the cold. He doesn't have the heart to go it alone on Treasure Island. How about we send him out to you for a month? This gives Cal and me a little break from having him here, Dad gets sunshine, and you get to have him in your home for your birthday." I loved the idea. San Diego seemed like as good a place as any to get Dad out of the bitter cold and ass-deep snow of Michigan.

Since Mom's funeral in October, Dad had been staying with Lynn and Cal. Each of us kids felt that he shouldn't be alone, at least until he rediscovered his ticking heart or decided to "check out," which was his favorite phrase for dying. I had been down, too, since Mom left. I lost my appetite and became super quiet, both very unlike me.

Desperate to lift my spirits, my loving husband had a plan of his own. Unbeknownst to me, the wheels were already in motion when Tom asked my dad to come and spend time with us to escape the cold. Tom knew I'd be so involved with Dad's care that I'd be oblivious to his secret plan. Lynn helped on her end, convincing Dad that it was imperative that he come out to see his baby girl turn 50. It was all set. The plan worked. Dad agreed to come out to San Diego and spend a month.

Behind the scenes, my husband pulled out all stops in a massive surprise birthday party undertaking. He thought that surrounding me with everyone I loved was just what the doctor ordered to shake me loose from my cocoon of sadness. What I knew, but did not have the courage to even whisper out loud, was that when Mom died, she took *more than one heart with her.*

CHAPTER ELEVEN

She Was Here

At first, my father and I didn't really know how to behave. We were both so empty and raw from our collective grief and the vacant space where our hearts used to be that we sort of just hovered around each other the first few days in this bizarre floating dance of rootless uncertainty. Eventually, we settled into a routine.

One morning after about a week, the kids were out the door to school and Tom was at work. Dad approached me and said, "I'd like to speak with your friend."

I said, "Which friend, Dad? I have a lot of friends. You're going to have to be more specific."

He said, "You know, that one that does séances and stuff."

"Ah, you mean my friend, Pam."

Over the years of being in California, my family, especially Mom and Dad, had adjusted to hearing about my unique friends with different lifestyles and interesting skills. Remarkably, they did not think I had lost my marbles, or at least they were polite enough to not say it to my face.

I explained to Dad that Pam was extremely busy, not to mention expensive. I told him I would at least ask and see if she would do a favor for me. I also told him that she was a very talented psychic, but I wasn't sure what he thought she could do to help him. Nonetheless, he seemed adamant that Pam held some sort of Holy Grail message for him and he needed to speak with her.

Dad had never met Pam. I had shared several stories of her fascinating gift along the way, that's all. But hey, who am I to deny my grieving 84-year-old dad a request to speak to my famous psychic friend? I called Pam and she said that she would absolutely take the time to speak with him. I assured her that it wouldn't be a long call, and we set it up for the following afternoon. It was a gorgeous, sun-streaked warm February that year. Since Dad was a huge sun worshiper, I set him up in the backyard with a lounge chair, ice water, and my landline.

I called Pam and introduced her to Dad. I then turned the phone over and went back inside to start prepping dinner. I gave them complete privacy. After 20 minutes or so, I peeked outside around the corner of the house. Amazingly, he was still on the phone. I let them be. I checked again 10 minutes later, and he was *still* on the phone. I was feeling somewhat guilty that I had stuck my friend—who makes very good money speaking with clients daily—on a free, very long call with my grieving dad. I was also extremely curious as to what was taking so long. Finally, after close to an hour, it appeared as though he was finally finished with their call. I came outside and walked up to him. I found my big bull of a dad sitting in the sun with tears streaming down his sun-kissed cheeks.

I immediately thought, *"Oh, no! Jane, what have you done?"*

I started apologizing profusely. I said, "I'm *so, so sorry,* Dad. I was only trying to help you, but it looks like I made a huge mistake."

Guilt-ridden thoughts ran through my head. *What the hell was I thinking? What a stupid idea! Why, oh why, did I arrange this call? Trying to help him, I had actually intensified his grief.*

Then he calmly said, "She was here."

I slumped down in the chair next to him and asked, "Who, Dad? Who was here?"

"Your mother. Your mother was here."

I started shaking all over. It was an involuntary shimmy that ran up and down my spine. Then he quickly stood up and said, "Come on, let's go listen. She is sending a recording to your studio."

My dad, who no longer moved fast, started bolting for the house like he was running a 50-yard dash. We both went to the garage where I have a small recording studio. Sure enough, Pam had emailed the recording of their call. I was incredulous. I had no idea she was going to go this far to help my dad in his heartbreaking grief, or even that she could connect with souls that had transitioned to The Next Room.

This proved to be the first of many manifestations with my mom. My mother was reaching out, and it was time to pay attention to what she had to say.

CHAPTER TWELVE

WHAT'S THE DEAL WITH THE DIMES?

It wasn't very long after my mother crossed over that I started finding dimes—everywhere and frequently. They appeared in random unexpected places and always alone. I found them inside the washing machine, the dryer, on my car seat, at Target, our church parking lot, in gas station parking lots, at the airport, and even in the middle of our bedroom floor. I've always been one to stop in the middle of the street to pick up a penny, no matter how dirty it appeared. So, when I started finding dimes, I was intrigued.

I didn't really understand why I was finding dimes or associate them with my mom until I met another psychic, Marisa Ryan. My boss at the radio station where I worked at the time informed me that he wanted to feature a medium for Halloween, so listeners could connect with their loved ones that had passed away. It sounded like fun. Marisa is a well-known psychic medium based out of Los Angeles. For several evenings, listeners called into the radio station and Marisa delivered messages from their loved ones that had moved beyond the physical realm. The phones were packed every night. As much as I wanted to talk to her at length about my mom, I knew she was here to do a job and provide entertainment for our listeners.

At the end of our shift, the two of us had a great exchange and she suddenly said, "Jane, your mother is leaving you dimes. I'm not sure why or what the significance is, but just know that those dimes you've been finding are from her. I don't know what she's trying to tell you by leaving them, but each time you find one, please know they're from her."

When I told my husband about Marisa's message, he suggested I start keeping the dimes together. I found a little black velvet bag to collect them, and soon my husband, children, and friends were finding them as well.

Have you ever had a dream come flooding back to you in the middle of the day? When it happened to me, it came with such a force and powerful feeling it was uncanny.

A week before my dad's birthday, I put together a happy package with all his favorite treats and birthday cards from every member of my family, even a card from our big old yellow Labrador, Honey. As I was standing at the counter to ship the package, the memory of a dream suddenly flooded over me. It was so overwhelming that I had to put my hands on the counter to maintain my balance and ground myself. In my vivid dream recall, my beautiful mother was sitting gently on the edge of my bed. I propped myself up in bed, and said, "Mom, what's the deal with the dimes?"

"I like to see you smile," she said.

There it was. The message was just like her—direct and to the point. I was filled with such gratitude and joy to finally find out the mystery of why my mother had been leaving me dimes. The message was so pure and simple it made me

WHAT'S THE DEAL WITH THE DIMES?

smile ear to ear. As I turned to leave, directly down at the toe of my right shoe was one bright, shiny dime! I burst out laughing, bent down, picked it up, and held it high in the air, all while smiling, laughing, and talking to my mother the entire time I walked out of the store. I giggled later that day thinking about everyone around me in the store and what they must have thought about the crazy woman holding a dime and talking to herself. I honestly didn't care one little bit. I now knew why Mom was leaving me dimes and it *made me smile*.

At work the following evening, I told my producer, JJ, about the dream that I had and the dime I found at my toe immediately after. He was with me as producer the evening that I had the exchange with Marisa.

"Are you writing it down each time you find one?" JJ asked.

I said, "No, that's a great idea. I will from now on!"

As I turned to reach for a note pad, something shiny caught my eye, underneath the console, way back in the corner. I crouched down to pick it up, laughing and smiling the whole time. It was one single, shiny dime.

As I presented it to JJ, he said, "Hi, Mom."

CHAPTER THIRTEEN

RUTHIE'S EYES

Besides all the dimes, and messages through Pam and Marisa, I started receiving other types of communication from my mom. The displays she sent me were getting deeper and more substantial and they were starting to exhibit a rather remarkable, other-worldly feel. I would not have believed what happened that day in my folks' kitchen, had I not witnessed it with my own eyes.

It was eight months after Mom's funeral. I had not seen my dad since he stayed in our home in San Diego during the month of February, trying to locate his beating heart. He needed to see me again, and I needed to see him. I flew home, picked up my sister, Lynn, and we headed north to hang out with Dad. We invited Bob and Ruthie Schlang over for cocktails and a visit. They lived just around the corner from my parents' home in Gaylord. Bob and Ruthie were, and still are, an intricate part of our family. They're often included in our family gatherings, from small cocktail parties to weddings and the occasional "pop in" for a visit. Bob is a staunch man who either likes you or he doesn't. You always know where you stand with Bob. Ruthie is a sweetheart and a gorgeous woman with vivid hazel eyes. She's also very intuitive and believes in angels and miracles. Bob, not so much.

While Dad, Lynn, and Bob chatted in the family room, I had a chance to catch up with Ruthie alone in the kitchen. She had been a solid foundation of support for me throughout my mother's entire hospital ordeal and transition. We were holding hands and looking into each other's eyes, our faces literally only five inches apart. I was telling her how much my mother loved her. And then it happened. A vivid blue vibrational light started pulsating through her eyes. I was so fascinated by this phenomenon, I calmly and quietly observed it for several moments.

When I finally spoke up, I said, *"Ruthie, you don't have blue eyes."*

She dropped my hands, spun around, and said, "Stop it, Jane, you are freaking me out!"

As soon as she dropped my hands, her eyes faded back to their natural hazel color. I apologized for tripping her out and explained that it was the coolest metaphysical thing I had ever experienced in my life. I shared with her precisely what I had just experienced, describing the pulsating, radiant blue light gently vibrating through her eyes. I even added sound effects for good measure. She knew immediately it was my mom.

I will never forget how it looked or, more importantly, how it made me feel. A peacefulness landed gently in my heart when this mystical manifestation occurred. I knew at that moment, without a shadow of a doubt, that my mother was letting me know she could see me, even if she had to use her best friend's eyes to deliver the message.

PART TWO
PAM

PART TWO PRAYER

Dear Heavenly Divine Energy of All—

I open my heart to receive.

Please grant me the ability to hear the messages that you would like me to share.

I also humbly ask for the understanding to articulate these lessons of my past with integrity, truthfulness, and grace.

In your name I pray,

Amen.

CHAPTER FOURTEEN

1983

I stepped off the plane and onto the enchanted soil of Santa Barbara, California. It was March of 1983. I had two suitcases and an old green trunk with all my earthly possessions from my 22 years on the planet nestled neatly inside. I instantly sensed that my life was about to shift dramatically. I felt a vibrational quiver on my skin as the scent of eucalyptus filled my nostrils and the site of the tall palms stretched toward the heavens. I could hear the faint whisper of a melody playing somewhere in the background as the vivid outline of the purple mountains hugged this magical place in a motherly embrace that only I could feel.

Even before I could see her, I felt her electricity swirling around me. It was the Pacific Ocean whispering my name as if she was urging me to come to her. I eagerly took the short ride from the airport to her shore. A salty reception beckoned me to come closer as her deep blue waves continued to roll in and out with a tender rhythm never to be duplicated. As if by a magical force, my shoes and socks flew off. She knew I was ready and gracefully eased up on the beach to greet me, placing a delicate blush of a kiss gently on the top of my wet sandy feet.

All my senses were keen and observant as my heart started pounding out a beat of gratitude, signaling a promise of something I had never experienced before. It was my intuition, rising to meet me at the water's edge.

CHAPTER FIFTEEN

MEETING PAM

By the beginning of 1983, I had already moved on to my third radio job in Petoskey, Michigan, when I received the call. The voice on the other end of the line was unmistakably that of radio legend Paul Christy asking me if I had ever been to Santa Barbara.

"No," I said.

"I haven't either, but I hear it's beautiful," he said.

That's the day I was asked to leave my family and my beloved Michigan for a once-in-a-lifetime opportunity to work at the fabled alternative rock radio station, KTYD, in Santa Barbara, California.

My invisible long-distance umbilical cord stretched as the airplane flew me farther and farther away from everyone and everything I knew and all that I loved. Until that day, I had never been farther west than Kalamazoo.

By the time I met Pam, my career had evolved into doing a morning show on KTYD with Terry Jaymes. Terry is a seeker, constantly raising his vibration and reaching out to unique and interesting people. Pam was already an established, well-known psychic in Santa Barbara, and she was Terry's latest fascination. They were friends. I was skeptical. To most people raised in the Midwest with traditional Christian values, what she was doing was considered devil's play. I honestly had no idea what a psychic actually did. I had never encountered one. I had no idea what to expect. Terry assured me that Pam would be good radio and asked me to try and suspend judgment.

I welcomed her on our show with what would be characterized more as curiosity than warmth. Pam was booked to spend the morning with us as we asked our listeners to call in with questions for her. Once we connected a caller with Pam, Terry and I would remain silent. Pam would ask the person on the phone the natural color of their hair and the color of their eyes. What followed was staggering. She told listeners very personal things about themselves that she had no way of knowing. Keep in mind, this was in the early 80s when Google was nothing more than someone's faraway dream. Pam had no way of researching the individuals that she spoke to on our show, as she told them her revelations immediately right there, "live" on the air. The things she shared that day ranged from upcoming surprise pregnancies to new jobs, health issues to be aware of, and even financial windfalls. Our listeners were amazed and I was intrigued. The next day, I decided to set up a private session with her. After the session, I left her home with my heart racing and my head spinning. The things she told me about my future life that day eventually happened. Every. Single. One.

CHAPTER SIXTEEN

CHICAGO

Pam's first prediction for me was a cross-country move and a career pivot. During my early days, radio was everything to me. I started my broadcast career when I was just 19. The first time I did an on-air show, I was hooked. I mean, come on, a profession that pays decent just for me to talk? I had found my calling. There were many perks as well, which included meeting and interviewing rock-and-roll stars, attending every concert with the best seats in the house, and all free. If that wasn't enough, all my drinks were on the house the second I walked into any bar. I had hit the jackpot! Many of my friends were also involved in radio. They were fun, inspired people with passion for music and a lust for life. I never even once considered doing anything else with my life. It was a dream occupation come true.

For my private session, I was invited to join Pam at her home in Santa Barbara. Everything in her place was white—the carpet, the walls, even her cat. The only other color I remember seeing was green. She had lots of plants. They were everywhere. Pam asked me to remove my shoes at the front door. I asked her about the white environment. She said it helped her to see auras. Auras? Oh man, I thought.

What the hell did I get myself into? Pam gave me over an hour of her time. I was in my mid-20s and only wanted to hear about my career, money, and travel. I was hoping she saw me at a big radio station in a major market with a large paycheck attached. That is what I wanted to hear. That is what I believed was supposed to happen next for me.

Santa Barbara had recently started to feel small. My ideas and dreams from childhood were still very much alive. The familiar feeling that I was put on the planet to do big things was still lurking in the shadows. I just didn't know what those big things would be. I was hoping this magic woman could tell me. Pam knew that I was born and raised in Michigan. That's about as much as she knew of me personally. I held my cards close to my chest and tried not to give her much information.

I wanted her to do all the talking that day. She told me she saw me back in the Midwest, but not Michigan. She then looked directly in my eyes and said, "Have you ever been to Chicago?" I told her, "No, never." She said, "Well, I'm seeing you in Chicago but not in radio, rather a career related to radio and music." I was deflated. I also thought to myself that her tuner was way off that day. First, I've never been to Chicago, and second, I didn't have one friend or relative living within a five-hour drive of the Windy City. I could not imagine moving back to the cold and snow, or, for that matter, getting out of radio. I thanked her and left her house feeling empty, and not sold on her so-called "fortune telling" abilities.

Two months later, I received a call from a guy I knew at Virgin Records. He asked if I had any interest in speaking with them about doing promotions and marketing. I thought I should at least hear what they have to offer, so I drove to Los Angeles to meet with him and his boss from Virgin Records.

As it turned out, the opening they had in mind for me was in Denver. They offered me the position on the spot. On the drive back to Santa Barbara, I smiled and giggled to myself about how far off Pam's predictions had been for me. I also started to visualize myself moving and living in Colorado. I didn't have much to go on. I had visited Denver once. I remember thinking how pretty it was with all the snow-capped mountains. That's all.

The next morning, the guys from Virgin Records called me. They said that they had a change in their offer. I listened. After I left the restaurant, they decided I was a strong enough candidate for a larger market than Denver. Then they asked me, "How would you feel about being the promotion record rep for Virgin Records working out of Chicago?"

I was stunned. I excitedly called Pam. "Guess where I'm moving?"

She calmly said, "Chicago."

Pam's intuition is astounding. It's as though she has an invisible antenna and she's tuned into her very own frequency that receives messages from a superior energy. She's like a little human radio station. Her channel seems to be mystically aligned with the great beyond. The day in my backyard when Pam met my dad over the phone was the precise moment that my understanding of her extraordinary abilities expanded. It was the day my mother started reaching out from beyond by leaving dimes or vibrating a blue light through her best friend's eyes. It was also the day Mom started to speak directly to us—from The Next Room.

CHAPTER SEVENTEEN

DAD'S SESSION WITH PAM

My dad moved swiftly across our living room with the tracks of his tears still visible on his warm cheeks. I settled him into my main chair in the studio and grabbed a small stool to pull up beside him. Just as Pam had promised, she had sent an audio recording of their call. Dad was as excited as a young kid being offered unlimited penny candy at the General Store.

This is a pivotal point in our story because it is the precise moment that I became aware that my mother could connect on a more substantial level. It was also a revelation for me regarding the tremendous level of talent that my friend Pam has in speaking with souls that have transitioned. My previous knowledge was that she could only see things. What I didn't know until that day was that she can communicate clearly with those on the other side.

The healing that occurred for my dad through Pam over his heartbreak of losing Mom was immediate, deep, and unprecedented. I'm in no way saying that a medium is preferable to grief counseling or seeking solace through your church or pastor. I'm just keenly aware that it worked miracles in my father's situation. Dad needed to know that my mother was okay and that she still loved him. He desperately needed to know that she was waiting for him just beyond the here and now in The Next Room. What's a daughter to give her dad who seemingly has everything except the love of his life by his side? In my case, the gift was a yearly phone session with my intuitive, gentle psychic medium friend, Pam Oslie.

What follows is an excerpt from the first session that my dad had with Pam. Out of respect for my father's privacy, I will only share the things that are pertinent to our story. Throughout the call, Dad remained quiet. He was tuned in and listening intently to what was being said while absorbing it all through his astonished silent tears of joy.

> *Don, I want you to know that I believe in free will. On some level, hopefully what I'm about to share with you will make sense to you. By the way, your wife Betty is here now. She's right beside you, literally jumping up and down because she is so excited to finally speak to you. Right off the bat, she wants you to know that you were a wonderful husband, a good father, and a great provider, and she couldn't imagine anyone better as her life partner.*
>
> *She is coming across as very heartfelt. She loves you very much and she's extremely grateful. She loved being your wife and the life you had together. She wants to know that she's sorry that she left. She did have an uneasy feeling about the surgery before, but she knows now it was exactly how it was supposed to be. She keeps repeating over and over and wants you*

to know she's filled with gratitude for the life she had with you. Don, Betty is really wanting me to express this next point to you.

She says, "You're not old, so please stop acting old. You still have a lot of gifts to give."

She doesn't want you just wandering around the house or putzing around the yard feeling lost. She doesn't like you just sitting around and being sad because she left. She feels you still have a lot to contribute. She is really emphasizing this next point. She wants you to know that you are not finished with life on this side. You will be around for several more years. Don, your wife is coming across very grateful for the life that you gave her and your children. She has so much love for you she is literally making me cry.

She is now telling me about her crossing and wants to share her experience with you. Her mother, dad, sister Alice, and her grandmother were all waiting for her. She wants you and your children to know that she's okay.

She did have a little intuition that she was going to have a challenge with the surgery, but she knew she had to at least try. She wants you to know that she truly, really loves you and appreciates you. She is repeating this message. She sincerely does not want you to feel lonely. She really doesn't like it when you are wandering alone, feeling empty and heartbroken. She is around you a lot, by the way. She loves being around you and the children.

Okay, this is so cute. She literally just started going around kissing each one of you in the family.

She said she couldn't have asked for a better life. She wants you to know that she's in Heaven now but that you gave her Heaven on earth. She is so dedicated to the family. She also has a very disciplined side. Does that make sense to you, Don? She's acting like a sergeant.

Dad laughed and told Pam that he often lovingly referred to Mom as "Sarge" because of her ability to run our family just like a sergeant runs a military unit.

CHAPTER EIGHTEEN

WWALD
(What Would Aunt Lynn Do)

It wasn't long after we buried Mom that we suffered another monumental setback in our family. My sister Lynn passed away from complications of cancer. In terms of time, it was six years. In terms of my heart, it felt like a beat. Aside from leaving me, she left behind her two grown sons, Chuck and Michael, whom she adored, and her faithful loving husband, Cal. Her departure was felt on a deeply essential level throughout her community, church, extended family, and hundreds of friends.

Lynn was a powerhouse of a woman and treated everyone fairly. She was what I would admiringly refer to as a mover and a shaker. In short, Lynn got shit done. There is no measurement for that pain, especially in losing someone like her, but I think of her daily and smile over the acronym she created—WWALD, which stood for, *What Would Aunt Lynn Do?* This important life lesson she taught my children was to pause, take a moment, and always think before reacting.

As I sat beside my Dad in church the day of her funeral, I sensed his bewilderment and could feel his excruciating grief over losing Lynn. I could literally feel his pain vibrating off his considerably large frame. I remember praying that I could somehow absorb even a fraction of his agony that day as he prepared to say goodbye to his beloved first born. The two of them were extremely close, and, if I'm being honest, I envied their relationship just a little.

Two weeks before Lynn died, I had taken Dad to the hospice facility where Lynn had been living out her final weeks. It was a dismal drive as we both knew we were going to see her for the last time, to say goodbye. As I steered him into her room, I gave them privacy and waited patiently just outside her room. When he walked out of the facility and away from Lynn for the last time, I guided him gently to the car and poured him into the passenger seat. When he could finally speak without crying, he shared with me his final words that he had spoken to her.

My dad described his yearly sessions with Pam as his "call to your mother." He looked forward to these visits with Mom and the date of his next scheduled call was quickly approaching just weeks after Lynn was laid to rest.

The following is a transcript from Dad's call with Pam after Lynn passed away.

Don, your wife Betty has much to share with you today, but she knows that you need to hear from your daughter, Lynn. She is stepping back so Lynn can speak with you first. First of all, Lynn wants you to know that she's doing great. She is now whole, complete, and free. She is watching over her boys and she is around them a lot. She has great love for both of her sons. Now she is looking directly at Jane. She is looking eye-to-eye with Jane and saying, "Thank you for all of your help." I feel like I want to cry when I say that. It was done with such love and sincerity.

Okay, Don, now she is smiling and emphasizing this next message. She's looking at you and saying, "Wow, what a ride, huh?" She's laughing when she says this and giving me the feeling that this is an inside joke. Does this make any sense to you?

With his voice shaking and on the edge of tears, Dad said to Pam, "That was the last thing that I said to her before I left her room." I told her, "We sure had a quite a ride."

It's no wonder she told me that, because there is no way I would have said that or used that phrase. Lynn just piped up and said, "Of course not, because I said that!"

Okay, Don, Lynn wants you to know she is doing fine, and you don't have to worry about her anymore. Your wife just added, "I've got Lynn and she is in the arms of the Lord."

Although it was a small exchange of words, they carried big meaning, and an ease settled on Dad's bronzed face. He had said "What a ride" in solitary confidence to Lynn while they were alone in her hospice room. Hearing those words again, through Pam, who lived 2400 miles away, seemed to give him further validation. He knew Pam was absolutely plugged into a direct line of communication to not only his soulmate, my mom, but to his first born and confidant—my sister, Lynn.

CHAPTER NINETEEN

"And Many More"

Dad always wore dark glasses and it pissed off my mom. She didn't like his curious green eyes being hidden. I didn't care. I thought he was cool. To me, it was his signature look. Imagine meshing Jack Nicholson and Burt Reynolds. That's what my dad looked like, except, in my opinion, much more handsome. Standing at 6'3" and 230 pounds, he was an imposing figure of a man.

Dad was always working when I was little. It was the sixties and he had six children to clothe and feed. He was up before sunrise to drive a Borden's milk truck, delivering fresh milk to all the people on his route in our small, rural town of Deckerville. After that, he'd jump into a Standard Oil gas truck and deliver fuel to farmers the remainder of the day. He worked every day except Sunday. He was home for dinner at 6 PM. Every night, all eight of us sat at the large kitchen table for a hot, home-cooked meal. I wonder if he ever stopped to eat lunch. I guess that's another great question for Pam. Funny, but it's all the little details that you don't know but want to know once they leave for The Next Room.

When I was around four years old, I'd stand by the huge sliding glass door in our big family room waiting for Dad to come home from work. I was a skinny little kid, with my brown hair cut in a short pixie with bangs. I have the same color green eyes as my dad. When he finally showed up, I was so happy that my heart started doing cartwheels and backflips. My hero—my big, sturdy dad—was home from another day of slaying the milk and gas dragons. I can still recall the smell of fuel oil on his clothes. Maybe that's why I am so fond of the smell of gasoline. Many times throughout his life, he described the scene of him coming home after another long day of working two jobs. He said no matter how difficult his day was, when he saw me standing there at the sliding glass door just waiting for him, all his troubles would evaporate, like a small puddle of water on a hot summer day.

Dad was a WWII vet. He joined the Navy when he was 16 and shipped out of San Diego. My grandfather had to sign papers giving a 16-year-old permission to enlist. Dad was on the USS Natoma Bay, CVE-62, when it was hit by a Kamikaze plane, killing an officer and injuring several others on board. Dad recalls hearing a huge boom as the plane crashed into them, blowing a large hole in the top of the ship. He was fond of reminiscing about his days in the Navy and had many colorful stories that included his best buddy, Lyle Milkerson. Years later, Lyle ended up being a groomsman in my folks' wedding.

Dad reveled in his birthday, which was February 7. He celebrated days before and continued right up to Valentine's Day, which he said was a natural cut-off. Dad held court wherever he was, and he loved receiving cards, gifts, phone calls, and his favorite treat, black licorice.

Leading up to his 91st birthday, I felt a strong desire to see him. I had not seen him since the summer before when I was in Michigan while he was in the rehab facility for his knee replacement surgery. I felt one of those undeniable hunches, or what I call a God wink. I just knew I had to see and be with him to celebrate his birthday.

I called my brother and told him I was going. I also told him that flights were inexpensive and suggested that maybe he should join me. If you ask him, he'll tell you that I got him in a headlock and insisted he join me. I remember it just a tad softer, more like a long-distance arm twist. After one more subtle call of encouragement, he gave me his credit card number and said, "Book it." Our plan was set.

We arrived in Tampa within minutes of each other—he from Detroit and me from San Diego. We grabbed our bags, hopped in an Uber, and off we went to Dad's one-bedroom apartment on the back water of Treasure Island. It was a super cute place with a split two-piece couch in the living room. This is where my brother and I slept for the entire week. We were cramped, but it was also hilariously perfect. I still snicker at the image of my 6' 3" big brother's legs hanging off his half of the couch. Dad seemed to get a huge kick out of having his two grown babies camping out in his living room that week.

My brother treated Dad and me to a lovely dinner the night before Dad's birthday. On our way in, we mentioned to the hostess that Dad would be 91. At the end of our meal, the waiter arrived with a slice of key lime pie, a lighted candle, and "91" written in whipped cream on the plate. All three of us sang Happy Birthday. When it came to the end of the song, Dad melodically sang, *"and many more."* The video I captured on my phone in that exact moment in time is now a rare and treasured gift.

The next day, on his actual birthday, we had a wonderful surprise visit. My cousin, Gary, who is also Dad's godson, showed up with his beautiful wife, Teri. Dad was elated. After an afternoon of reminiscing and cocktails at Dad's place, we headed over to the beach and kept the party going. Dad's favorite—the Dixieland Jazz band—was playing that night. We had a ball singing, dancing, and watching the joy vibrate off my dad's face. As I watch the video of him singing "When the Saints Go Marching In," while waving his white napkin, I see it as another sign. Here was my big daddy enjoying life to the fullest with a handful of his favorite people at his favorite place, listening to his favorite music—all while waving a white flag.

The following day, the celebration continued with a cocktail party attended by his Florida pals and neighbors. We had all kinds of food from a local deli and the adult beverages were flowing. Dad was in his element with his three youngest children by his side—me, Tom, and Donna, who lived nearby. Dad was center stage all afternoon while the three of us served food, refreshed drinks, snapped pictures, and celebrated his first full day of entering a new year. Little did we realize at the time, there would not be *"and many more"* to his story. Just 43 days later—he checked out.

CHAPTER TWENTY

Get Busy Living

My big, strong, tenacious and frequently opinionated father left to join his best friend, my mom, on March 22, 2018. It was a mere seven years, five months, and 21 days since she had exited this life as we know it, taking his heart with her. I still smile over what my bestie, Nancy, said when I called her that day to tell her how dad had passed away. She said, "Big Don stuck the landing." To this day, I quote her when I tell the story of how my dad quietly slipped into The Next Room while sitting in his chair in front of the TV. He always lived so large, and for him to manifest such a peaceful, easy departure was—in my opinion—flawless.

After my mother left us, I thought Dad may decide to follow right behind her. It seemed as though he had given up on life. He was bewildered and sad, and he would often ponder out loud as to why she left before him. It was evident to each of us who deeply loved him that he didn't really care to navigate life on his own. He was fond of using the depressing phrase, "I'm just marking time." It sucked to hear him throw in the towel. I got after him repeatedly, reminding him that he was here because he wasn't done learning, sharing, and growing as a human being. I told him many times that he would be reunited with my mom soon enough. To drive the point home, I would quote my favorite line from the movie, Shawshank Redemption: "Get busy living or get busy dying." I understood that they were balanced souls and that he missed her, but honestly, it pissed me off to hear him talk that way.

All of his children and grandchildren rallied around him, each of us available for him in our own unique ways. He heard many of us telling him over and over that his journey was not complete and that we needed him to stick around. We encouraged him through countless visits and phone calls, asking for his sage advice. And through the assistance of Pam, my mother continued to nudge him to engage with the family, get out of the house, stay active, and for the love of all things holy, to stop being a downer about her leaving before him.

After the initial shock and without his heart, he marched on. Many times, it appeared that he was turning a corner. He seemed to thrive as long as he had people around. It didn't matter if it was family, a neighbor, his housecleaner, or the plumber. He would light up in any conversation. From the age of 83 to 90, Dad was still in relatively good health. He was vibrant and had every single marble firmly in place, although sometimes rolling on a repeat loop.

In the space in time from Mom leaving this life to his death, he stopped moping and got busy living. Besides traveling to San Diego to celebrate my surprise 50th birthday party and staying with us for a month, he added many more miles and years of fun to his life. He returned to Florida for several winters. He flew back to San Diego for our daughter Betty's high school graduation and two years later for our son Thomas'. He witnessed the births of his fifth and sixth great grandchildren, Jackson and Peter James. I can still hear his throaty chuckle and see the look of pure joy as he would let those little boys crawl all over him in his favorite chair—and even touch the remote. One of his most cherished honors arrived when he was asked by my niece Carey's fiancé, Sean, to be a groomsman in their wedding. Although moving a little slower, he soldiered on, even with a bad knee. So, what should a 90-year-old do with a bum part? Most people would request a wheelchair and sit it out. Not Dad. He decided to have knee replacement surgery. Yes, at 90.

On one hand, it's too bad he didn't get to put his new knee to more use. On the other hand, at least he enjoyed one more . . .

One more trip to the beach.

One more foot rub.

One more set of Dixieland music.

One more plate of oysters on the half shell.

One more rum and Diet Pepsi.

One more workout at the gym.

One more communion at church.

One more sunrise.

One more sunset.

One more birthday.

And one more "I love you, Dad."

CHAPTER TWENTY-ONE

My Journal Entry from Thursday, March 22, 2018

It took you to die for me to pick up my pen. I have been bewildered for eight years with wandering thoughts and rudderless direction. This story that is etched in my spirit lacks the oxygen it craves to breathe, so it can finally wake up and come alive. But now, you're dead. I am pinched off by uncertainty, abstract fear, and my resistance to face the truth. Through my torrent of tears, I begin to write. You left today. You checked out. You entered The Next Room. I envision you, in this moment, strong, vigorous, and free—without an ache or a pain. Hundreds of conversations flood through my thoughts, each one vivid, distinct, and telling. They crash into me, like the raging Pacific Ocean against the California shoreline on a blustery winter day. All my memories start piling up faster than laundry after a two-week vacation. The awareness of your death seeps in through my pores as it pushes me deeper down into my dejected corner of brokenhearted melancholy. I can't breathe. I reach for the spot where my kind heart used to reside—now empty, my chest delicate to the touch. I feel bruised, battered, and broken, as if I were placed in a boxing ring without gloves or the energy to fight back. I miss you. You were not only my father. You were my friend, and guiding light. Who's going to illuminate my path, now that you're not here to shine your light?

CHAPTER TWENTY-TWO

Dad's Crossing

Over the years and many times before Dad died, we would have spirited conversations about the afterlife and what we both thought would come next. Ever since he started having yearly conversations with my mom through Pam, he took comfort and had renewed confidence that he would indeed be reunited with her when his time came. I also teased him by asking him to leave me hundred-dollar bills. I assured him that I would be connecting with him through Pam, but that I would give him plenty of time to gain his sea legs, so to speak. In typical Dad fashion, he replied, "What makes you so sure that I'm leaving before you?" As it turns out, he did.

The following is transcribed from my session with Pam, approximately two months after Dad checked out of here and into The Next Room.

Just let me repeat what your dad told me just before you called. When he went to the other side and he saw your mom, he had tears of joy. He was unbelievably, ecstatically happy when he saw her.

Your mom is so cute, Jane. She was hugging him and holding him, all while telling him, "See, I told you I was here." It was a very happy reunion and your dad said he got more than he bargained for, because not only was your mother waiting for him, he also saw his mom and dad, your mom's folks, his brother, your Uncle Doug, his sister, Aunt Marian, and of course, your sister Lynn! He also saw some of his loved ones who had crossed a long time ago that he had sort of forgotten about. It was a very blessed reunion.

Okay, now your mom is right here, and she wants you to know that she is proud of you for starting the book. She's showing me that she's right next to you and ready to go when you are. She also said you don't have to worry about your dad, he is in God's hands. They are all together. They are all there, even Honey. Aw, Jane, your mom is going to make me cry. She just hugged you and said, "Thank you for taking care of your dad. All of you kids did a good job." He was well taken care of. So please, no regrets now. She's got him. She's holding him by the hand. Jane, this gesture of your mother's was done with such overwhelming love and gratitude it's making me cry.

She also said she was front and center when he crossed and that she had to be the first one to see him or he would have been disappointed. She said when he left it was easy. He just stopped breathing, his heart stopped and then he was on the other side. She wants all of you kids to know that it really wasn't a struggle for your dad at all. He dozed off watching TV and he thought he was dreaming of her, but she was really there, calling him home. When he actually saw her, he was so happy.

Your dad just chimed in and said he felt like he had a little pinch. But he didn't even notice or care because he was so enthralled to see your mother again. Your mom helped guide him over easily and gently. Your sister, Lynn, was there, too, waiting and ready to welcome him home. I'm asking your dad if he wants to talk to you but he's deferring to your mom. He said she's better at this. By the way, he's younger. He looks like he's around 50 years old.

Now he is speaking up and telling me this loud and clear. He really loves you, Jane. He is so happy, he's almost speechless. That's why he was letting your mom talk—because she's more practiced at this. He is saying that he is not concerned about what he left behind. As much as he loved everything about their home, it just wasn't the same after your mother had left. It had lost its shimmer. He's very happy and content where he is right now. He really loves your mother's mom—your grandmother, Emma—and his brother, Doug. He just looked right at you, Jane, and said, "Don't let this be a struggle." This is in reference to the things he left behind for you kids. He is calling it the leftovers. He is so happy. He's with the love of his life. He actually just said, "Many lives."

Okay, Jane, he's really talking now. He just said, "I hope you have fun writing the book. It's a good book and I'm happy you're finally writing your story with your mom. Please continue to write the book; it is an important story to tell." He sees it even more so, now. He's admitting that he wasn't quite sure when he was alive, although he was supportive of you and your idea, but he didn't really understand if it was really true or if it was just your fantasy. He now knows for certain that it's all real. He says, "Get it done." He believes you will, and he hopes a lot of people read it. He wants you to know that he fully supports you and believes that this story will help a lot of people.

PART THREE
ME, MOM & PAM

PART THREE PRAYER

I walk, I pray, I stop.

I cast my face to the open sky.

As I gaze up at the blue skies that are alive with faraway clouds,

I say—

"Dear God, what is it that you would like me to know?"

A tender message rises up to greet me—

Legions of spiritual beings that have flown alongside you, have been waiting patiently for you to ask for their assistance. You are here to live your life's purpose, and to be guided as you open hearts and minds. This offering will ease grief, and teach peace, love and understanding. Your intention was designed in the stars, so let it shine. Those dreams you had as a young girl, have never left you.

You may have overlooked them or possibly hid them along with the treasures you buried beneath the soil by the old tree in your backyard. They are pleading with you now to be dug up and released.

Fill your lungs with a deep breath of desire and allow your fingertips to dance across the keyboard spilling forth your message of truth. The understanding of centuries of sages that came before you—are alive. The tears that well up in your eyes, they are your advisor. When they arrive without hesitation, may they fill you with the anticipation of what's to come. Let this magnitude of passion be your north node.

And so, it is.

Amen

CHAPTER TWENTY-THREE

RIGHT HERE—WRITE NOW

She whispered to me from The Next Room.

Write what's in your heart.

Don't worry about getting it right, you can't possibly get it wrong.

You see, my little one, it's the continuation of a never-ending love story.

My story. Your story. Our story.

The story of ALL beings.

They are connected, guided, protected, and wrapped in a universal blanket of love woven from the softest cotton of our memories.

Years, lifetimes, and moments all blend into one now, right here—

Write Now.

CHAPTER TWENTY-FOUR

All the Signs

Sometimes we need a little push, or, in my case, a firm shove in the desired direction. It's an odd thing to say, but I'm going to say it anyway. I feel that my father needed to, in his words, *check out*, before this story could be told in its entirety. Now that I have his belief and blessing, I feel I can continue with writing.

I have carried a deep yearning to write a book about the captivating bond I shared with my mom. I didn't know what form it would take or, for that matter, how to even write a book. After years of excessive talking, I decided to stop yacking about it and finally sit down and dedicate myself to actually writing it.

All the signs—the dimes, the vibrating blue light in Ruthie's eyes, and the pearls of wisdom Mom peppered throughout her sessions with Pam over the years—were pleading for a proper outlet. At the supernatural suggestion from my big sister, Lynn, I contacted Pam, who graciously agreed to assist me in communicating with Mom, just as she had done over the years for Dad.

CHAPTER TWENTY-FIVE

Into a Greater Awareness

The following is a transcript of my first session with Pam and Mom.

Pam   Your mom is right here. She is saying, "Okay, okay, let's go. There's no time to waste." She's also saying, "Great job." She's proud of you. One second, she gets right down to business and then she says something funny and then she's right back to business. She is charming, warm, loving, and happy. She says she has been very busy over there. She has grown a lot. She is very busy. I asked her, "Busy doing what, Betty?" She says, "Well, I'm helping, I'm learning. I'm traveling. I'm doing things." She says she is talking to people. She is helping out as part of a team. They are helping others.

She is so cute. Seriously, your mom is quick-witted. She is bright and just said she has gotten wiser over there. I was going to say smarter, but she said "wiser." She has become more aware—more, I want to say, more tuned in. Oh my gosh. For some of this stuff, Jane, there are no words. She is using words like obvious, obvious education. She says you get over there and realize, "Oh, of course that's how it is."

She keeps saying she has been very busy. She can do all kinds of things simultaneously over there. She is very happy. She's saying to you, "Let's go let's go let's go." She is wiser, more expansive. Every time I start to say smarter, she says "wiser." She's more aware, more in sync, more conscious, more . . . I can't hear the word but I know what it is. It is beyond every word I just spoke. More . . . not more intelligent . . . more . . . it's . . . oh, I like that term . . . she just called it Spiritual Intelligence.

Jane   I like that.

Pam   Spiritual Intelligence. I have never heard that phrase before, but that's what she is calling it. It's the best way to describe it. This awareness, it's a more expansive understanding. These are her words, Jane. I haven't heard these words put together like this before. But I can tell what she means by it. It's a broader scope of understanding of the universe. I'm going to say it that way. She said it's remarkable. It's wonderful. It's fascinating, and it's intriguing because it all fits together. All the pieces fit. Whenever you think things in life are fragmented, you look at the bigger picture and there is always a larger purpose and it all fits together. And she is just enamored by that. You know, like little fragments of glass on the ground are not really pieces but part of a greater whole. You get to have this understanding from a brighter and broader perspective.

It's weird because I know I'm not quite using the right words, but she is showing me the energy. Then you see it and you know that the glass wasn't really shattered at all. All those pieces fit together perfectly. The phrase she's using is, "There is a purpose for everything." And she is using the word understanding. She doesn't mean a small word understanding. She means a big all-encompassing understanding. You see how it all fits together. It's all synchronistic. It's all harmony. It's like when you have a little alignment moment. She said magnify that 10,000-fold and then you will see the universe and the magnificence of the synchronicity. It's beyond any words that we have. It's all purposeful.

She wants to show you how grand the experience was—how much she has gained a Spiritual Intelligence. And she has gained a spiritual understanding beyond . . . oh my gosh, your mom is quoting the Bible. She has seen a truth that surpasses all doctrine and all understanding. It is bigger than words can express. She said it's beyond comprehension and yet you know it all. You sense it all. You know it's the truth, but you are continuously expanding into a greater awareness—one that surpasses all understanding.

CHAPTER TWENTY-SIX

Beyond Love

As I'm asking questions in the dialog below, Mom is speaking through Pam. Pam is also providing comments on her own.

Jane   Mom, please tell me about The Next Room.

Mom   You can stop what you are doing at any phase and do whatever job, whatever project you want. You can talk to people about philosophical ideas.

Pam   She's telling me that she has spoken to some of the great masters, artists, writers, philosophers. She's been able to sit with all of them and listen to them speak.

Mom   It is like when you go to a book talk.

Pam   She says you'll be doing that, by the way.

Mom   It's learning-expansion, Jane. Those two words go hand in hand, they are connected.

Pam   She's really enjoying herself on the other side. She is emphasizing this point.

Mom   It's a very expansive awareness of infinite proportions, and they haven't even touched on Infinity because it just keeps expanding. There's always more to learn, more to experience, more to know. You can stop what you're doing at any time and help someone on this side. You can help them transition, help them to get off drugs, help people that are grieving deeply, like the loss of a child, sort of like a guardian.

Pam   She is describing it as rooms, although they are not actual rooms. She knows that you use The Next Room to describe your experience with people that have transitioned, and she likes that. She's describing her experience in rooms and, in doing so, puts the experience of what's next in a comprehensibility that most people can understand.

Mom   I like The Next Room as a descriptor as it is accessible and practical, and it makes sense to people that may have trouble comprehending an unending eternity. Imagine that you're in a room, and over in this room is your dad, and in another, your sister, and over here is the grand lecture hall. You can just go in and listen to the discussion, but there are really no rooms at all, unless you want to create it that way.

Jane   I'm happy she likes the visual of The Next Room. That description was given to me by my dear friend, Budgie. Okay, next up. Let's talk about God. Is it love, is it a being, or is it an energy?

Pam   This is going to be tricky because she said it's hard to put it into words but God is everywhere. It's a very expansive feeling. It's bigger and grander than anything you can imagine or even begin to describe in words. She really wants you to get this feeling.

Mom   God is everywhere. There are no boundaries, no stopping of God, skin doesn't stop it, walls cannot stop it.

The second word she is using is love. God is an uncon-ditional cherished treasure of big, bold, gooey love that warms you from the inside out and makes you realize the grace and goodness of God as everything. It's a fatherly love, but not in a gender sense, rather like the attributes of a father, like a grandfather who is continually taking care of everything. It's beyond love.

Jane   How do you go beyond love?

Mom   It's deeper than words, in all its forms, all of its ex-pressions, all of its manifestations. It's not one being, it's many beings. It's all comprehensive.

Pam   Your mother is a smart woman. She's using descrip-tions and words that I don't normally use. She's become smarter. She's letting me use the word smart now.

Jane   Laughs.

Pam   Smart in the way we would understand. She's gained more insight, awareness, comprehension, expansion, and wisdom.

Jane   So, God is all that and more?

Mom   You want to talk about God? It's everything, Jane, all that and more. It's love, love, love, all love. God doesn't have forms, but it takes forms, because it is everything.

Jane   So, when we are in these physical forms, why do we limit ourselves?

Mom   Intentionally, for the experience. It's a unique experi-ence. Don't worry about those that may be offended by the way you choose to describe God, because there are souls out there that will find the excuse to be offended by anything. You must write from your heart, write from your understanding

Pam   She likes that she gets to co-author this book. It's meaningful to her.

Jane   I will write from my heart, and I will stay with my integrity. I am honored that we are co-authoring our book. It is deeply meaningful to me as well.

Mom   What else are you curious about?

Jane   Is there a way to expand our consciousness and grow while we are still on this side?

Pam   Your mom is blowing up a balloon right now.

Mom   Yes. It's already happening. We get exclusionary. It's like you're looking at life through a little hole in a cardboard box and that's all you see. You think it's all there until you pull your face away from the box, and then you say, "Oh, Oh, OH—now I get it." That's basically what death is.

Pam   She likes the box analogy. I've never had anyone show me this before, but here is what I'm seeing. I'm looking at a little hole in a cardboard box, like a shoebox with a lid. She's showing me that the walls are getting thinner, you know like in the Bible it says the veil is becoming thinner. With this box, the walls are getting thinner or transparent, so people are getting glimpses. The box is getting see-through and there really is no lid on the box. We choose to have a lid on it, almost like, "Don't lift up the lid on the box because then I won't have the experience of what's inside this box." No one has ever shown me that example before. It's really cool. So, Jane, imagine looking in the box and thinking, "This is reality.

There's Europe, there's Africa, there's America, there's the politics, look at this, look at that." With our limited understanding, we can only see what's in our box, and everyone's box holds a different life experience. With death, you finally pull away from looking in the box through the little hole and you see that it was just a box. God doesn't want us to look in a box for eternity, so death lets us return to a greater perspective. Ha! I like your mom. She's showing me a whole bunch of little guys with boxes all over the place, like different eras. It's been happening over eons of time, if you're going to use the term "time."

Jane   I love this visual. It also really makes sense to me the way she is describing our life experience. Each one of us only sees what's right in front of us in our own little box.

CHAPTER TWENTY-SEVEN

Jesus and Spiritual Paths

Pam   So, what else would you like to know?

Jane   What about Christianity? Even though she and Dad
        raised us Christian, and I'm a big fan of Jesus and his
        compassion for all beings, I have felt for a very long
        time that Christianity is too limiting for a society
        with a multitude of spiritual paths and religions. We
        have so many deep ways to reach for a more com-
        prehensive understanding of God. You know, many
        doors to Heaven.

Mom   It's a limited perspective. They all are. Everything
        that we experience here is designed to have limited
        perspective, except love. Love doesn't have limita-
        tions but everything else does.

Pam   I just asked her, "What about hate?"

Mom   Limitations. Love has no boundaries, hate does.
        Hate won't last, because it is limited. Love is the eter-
        nal creative force of life.

Pam   I just got goosebumps.

Mom   Don't judge the different perspectives, because they
        are all meant to add to what is.

Pam   Jane, your mom is saying things I've never heard before, it's so cool to hear.

Mom   Imagine them as secret societies, like little secret groups on a playground and they all have their little cliques, and yet when you go back into the classroom in The Next Room everybody is here together learning the same lesson once again.

Pam   Why are you referring to them as secret societies?

Mom   It's because they all think they have the secret while they are here on Earth. It's as though they think their truth is the only way. However, there are billions of them.

Jane Okay, so while someone is here on this plane, they have their own version of what they believe, or what their own secret society believes. So, when we transform and cross over, are we then aware of our grander purpose?

Mom   Most people, yes. However, some souls are stubborn. Most people pull away and recognize that they were only viewing what was in their box. Occasionally, someone will not want to see the illusion. It doesn't last long because it becomes a freedom. The stubbornness is just their limiting fear and it's rare.

CHAPTER TWENTY-EIGHT

Elevated Souls and Forgiveness

Jane   I'm curious about the highly elevated souls that are here with us now on this earthly plane, like the Dalai Lama.

Mom   They chose their roles, and on the other side too. There are different levels. But here on this side they have chosen their roles to be spiritual leaders to help people. Sometimes they are even encouraged to play that role because they have had experiences that make them elevated enough to understand. It's like a soul that is a college graduate versus one with a five-year old's understanding. Can you imagine a five-year old trying to run a church or a country? They are too young in their understanding and then would get lost and just have temper tantrums.

Jane   What about people who have harmed and hurt others?

Mom   That is not a grand soul. They got distorted along the way. They were tampered with and they just simply got off track.

Jane   Is there still a level of forgiveness with these individuals? You know, like when someone does something atrocious and you hear the words, "That person should burn in hell."

Mom   It's all forgiveness, Jane. It's all forgiveness because it is hand in hand with love. It's all forgiven, and it is all understood because once you understand something there's no need for forgiveness.

Jane   What about hell?

Mom   It's an illusion in mankind's mind. It's man's self-made, self-restrictive prison. It was created by certain souls to try to keep themselves in line and they passed it down to everyone else. It was created by souls that didn't trust themselves when they got here. They were scared and didn't know what to do so they started making rules up because they didn't trust, and it was unfamiliar.

Pam   She's got me in a classroom where everyone is being shushed . . . be quiet, be quiet . . . we have to behave ourselves.

Mom   Bottom line, hell is not real. It's in man's mind. They created their own hell.

Pam   She keeps showing me a box.

Mom   It was designed that way for the experience. Almost like in the 20s or 30s when they would show a movie. You had to look through a box to watch the movie.

Pam   Was your mom born during that time?

Jane   Yes, 1927.

Pam   No wonder she is showing me an old-school projector of a movie to describe our life experience in that type of a box.

Mom   Everyone is saved. There's no one lost on the other side. It was never broken.

Jane   This gives me comfort. Okay, another question. When I see someone on a street corner and they are asking for money, I give it to them. I don't judge whether or not they should be asking for it or what the reason is that they are asking for it. My thought is if I have it to give, why not give it? I have been chastised for doing that.

Pam   Yes, like they might go buy drugs or alcohol.

Jane   Yes, if I have something to give and someone needs something, I feel I should share it.

Mom   There is no should. You choose to share your money. It's all choice, honey, and not only is it choice but it's all grace. No one is punished for the choices they make. They are not judged for wanting to do or experience different things.

Jane   I feel we are all here to help one another.

Mom   We are. It's fun, Jane. It's interesting and challenging, but there's fun in these challenges. It's all alive, it's eternal. Nothing disappears, nothing dissolves, including the animals, even little ants or little starfish. It's all eternal. They may change forms, but they still exist.

CHAPTER TWENTY-NINE

CONNECTIONS
AND GUIDANCE

Jane   Mom, what about the connections we have here? It's interesting to me how much deeper some relationships are, such as my connection to you. I have never felt more aligned with another person. It's been almost a decade and I still feel the loss on a deep level.

Mom   It's by design. That familiarity and love for one person or another is because they have journeyed together before. You decided to go look at that same box together in another lifetime. We all get to choose whatever we want to do because it all is and there's no judgment about any choices we make because it is all grace. It's almost like asking a child which color of candy they want. You wouldn't judge them for their choice.

Jane   Wow, that is so good.

Mom   Some people get lost in their fear and tangled beliefs about who they are and how reality works. When they come back here, sometimes it takes them a little longer to untangle because they got delusional in the illusion. It may take them a little while to get a grasp on what's real and remember that what they experienced in the physical was their interpretation of reality and not reality itself. There is no judgment because it's all grace.

Jane   What about forgiveness?

Mom   There's no need for forgiveness here, but if you're going to use the word forgiveness, you need to know that it literally means For Giving. This experience is for giving to you. It's for your benefit, a way to experience balance and ease.

Jane   When I cross, will I see things that I could have done better, and will I have any regrets?

Mom   Regrets are not true. When someone crosses, they do not have regrets. You get to see and review personally everyone that you were connected to in your life, the good, the bad, the ugly, the love, the caring. It's a life review. Let go of the word regret. It's not the appropriate word for it. A better word is insight—insight with love and compassion. There is no judgment. That's another church misperception. It's a life review with understanding, insight, aha moments, compassion, and love.

Jane   When I specifically ask for guidance from a soul that has gone before me, even one I personally have not met, do they hear me? Are they able to assist me in showing me the way, to guide me to a better outcome?

Mom   The first thing I want you to know is that it comes from everywhere and anywhere. It comes from the collective. It comes from God or Source. It comes from wherever it is needed. There are specific entities that do hear you and if they can help, they will. If it's not theirs to answer or not their forte, another being will step in to answer. It doesn't matter where it comes from. What matters is that you hear the right answer.

Jane   Whoa, that is goose-bumps good. Thank you so much, Mom. I really, really love your explanation. Would you please describe your personal crossing over into the Next Room in detail?

Mom   Once I let go, the final let go, it was delightful. It was blissful, unconditional love. Your dad was there in the room with me, so I didn't quite let go at first. I thought it would be impolite to leave him behind. Once I allowed myself to let go, it was like flying and floating that you've never experienced before, yet you have multiple times, you just forgot. It was easy and free.

Pam   Jane, your mother is giving me chills all over my body as she is illustrating this.

Mom   It was a love that was so big, so huge, so real, so fulfilling, a love that I had forgotten how to experience, even though I had loved full-on when I was there. It was beyond any kind of love that I had experienced on that side. It was more expansive. It was like floating in the air with not a care in the world. It is magical, beautiful, and ecstatic. It is beyond the word love as understood on your side. It's God Love.

Pam   She's trying to help me experience it and really feel it but she knows I'm limited because I'm still in my body and in my present mind consciousness.

Mom   It's an expanded state of love-filled awareness, alive-ness, or being-ness. It's the feeling that I Am Love. I was surrounded by it and realized I've never been apart from it. I also was able to identify familiar souls and some that were important to me but I had forgotten about. It is the realization that this is the truth of who we really all are. It's all one, and yet we have the ability and permission to come into a denser individual form in order to connect and communicate in a way that you can recognize.

Pam   You know, Jane, I have not heard this come through before from anyone. I love that you're asking your mom these types of questions because she's able to describe her experience in her own way so that it makes sense to me. I like it.

Jane   Pam, I'm so grateful that she would share such a beautiful moment as her crossing. I feel so fortunate that she made you feel this expansive love. What a gift.

Pam   It was phenomenal to experience that through her.

CHAPTER THIRTY

Expand with No Fear

Jane   I'm curious—if and when organized religions will catch up with this type of thought consciousness that we are all connected, or won't they?

Pam   Your mom is so cute. Check this out. She is showing me a three-prong answer to organized religions catching up with this thought. She says: 1) They already are; 2) It already is caught up on a certain level; 3) Never.

Jane   How can this be?

Mom   Because there are different layers. There are certain religions where the people involved need their rules. You know, "Give me the steps." People in those realms are happy with where they are in their belief systems. In other areas the expansive thought is already present and in others some are experiencing an awakening and starting to catch up. There are different levels of understanding. The necessity is based on the soul's need and their journey.

Jane   This leads me to my next question. The Bible. It was obviously written by man, but is it God's true message for us?

Mom   It's not the entirety of God's true message. There are many pearls of wisdom in there. There are elements of God in the Bible because God is everywhere. But let it go, don't even worry about it. Expand beyond because it has been colored by man. It's not God's full story. It is man's level of understanding at that time in history. It's not the full story or the full glory of God, which could never be contained in just one book. The bottom line is, the word of God, the energy of God first and foremost, is in your heart, your soul, your being-ness. So, go there. That's where God resides.

Jane Wow, this is really a great explanation of God's message. There's no possible way to capture the magnitude of the love in mere words.

Pam   Yes, exactly. She says, what else would you like to know?

Jane What is it that she would like me to know, that perhaps I'm not getting or that I haven't figured out just yet?

Pam   These are her words for you.

Mom   Expand with no fear, Jane. Let go of the fear, let go of the mental state, let go of the constrictions, let go of the restrictions, let go of thinking about it so much.

Pam   Expand into a state where it's all allowing. She is using the words "channel this information." Your mom is saying this with love, by the way. None of this is judgment. It's observation. She said you get stuck in your head about things. You come from your heart, but you do get stuck in your head occasionally. You want to do a good job and she's proud of you, she appreciates that she loves you for that, but it limits you. She keeps saying expand with no fear, expand without boundaries, expand into the greatness of it. She just said again that you'll be able to channel the information without my assistance. She wants to make sure she didn't offend me. Honestly, Betty, that was no affront to me, I didn't take it that way. Jane, if you expand into that glorious state of grandness of that arena, then she'll be able to communicate with you directly. Which she already does by the way, it's just that sometimes you pass it through your head or your thoughts. She said you're getting there, you're getting better. She wants you to allow yourself to be expanded and carried out to a greater connection and then the words will come to you. The book will be channeled through you.

Mom   It's important that people experience the grace of God. The beauty that's involved in the grace and the grandness of the all-seeing, all-knowing, all-being. It's so expansive, so beautiful, so grace filled that if people understand this feeling of expansive love they will never, ever be afraid again in their life. They would feel and know that God supports them with the expansive all-encompassing unconditional love.

Pam   She wants you to know that there's more to come and she can talk to you directly, if you'll allow it. She wants the fullness of the experience, the emotion of it to come through. She wants the essence of her answers to come through the book.

Jane   I want that as well. I have never stopped talking to her since the second she crossed. I'm just hoping and praying that I can hear what she has to say without your assistance, Pam.

Pam   Jane, she is absolutely certain that you do not need me to write your book together. Here's what she is reiterating to me.

Mom   You can hear me, sweetheart. You and I have actually been communicating for years. You do not need anyone's help to connect with me. But you must get out of your own way. And I will say this again, so it sinks in. Expand without fear, Jane. Be still and allow our communication to flow.

CHAPTER THIRTY-ONE

Checking In

I scheduled a call with Pam to check in with Mom. I didn't want to ask my mother any more questions through Pam. I just felt the need to connect to see if Mom felt I was aligned and on target with what I had been writing of our story thus far.

Jane I want to be sure that it's not just me coming through and writing. You know—my ideas, my thoughts, and my energy.

(Mom, through Pam)

 Of course not! We are writing this together, we are coauthoring, so your words and your thoughts also matter. Don't discount your thoughts, your feelings, your beliefs, your messages. As a matter of fact, you're the voice of those of us on this side.

Pam And by the way, your mom is telling me that she's not the only one helping you over there.

Mom There are legions of beings that want these messages to come through, to help people, to give them hope, to give them faith, to give them joy and to help them not be afraid of life, to not be afraid of death, to have positive reinforcement and know that they are loved. They know that you are doing great. You are doing the highest level of integrity that you know how to do, and they are all appreciating you for it. It's to be understood that the frequency comes through the screen of human understanding. Don't expect that everything must be perfect. The world of perfection is at such a high level that very few, if any, will understand it from this plane. All you have to do is speak human, talk to the humans here, talk to the people here, be real, be authentic—loving and authentic. Those are your words, and then bring the light. That's all that's required of you. They don't expect perfection because the human language won't understand it. The level of transcendence on this side is so high there's no way you could translate it into a mere book. Many have tried.

Pam   She's pointing at the Bible.

Mom   Even that beloved book has misunderstandings and human foibles in it. Just bring the light. Open your heart and transcribe. Bring the light and come from authenticity. That's all that's expected of you, that's all you can do, and you're big-time appreciated for that. Don't worry if you're doing this right or if it's perfect. It's not possible, sweetheart, not possible. Even the holy books were translated through human understanding and filters. And it's all fine. It's the intention and the overall message and theme that come through. The perfection is not in the words. It's the energy, the love and light. Never mind the perfection of each individual word. If you only understood the blanket of frequency of love, of calm, of comfort, and nurturing. It's under the umbrella of higher light, higher witnessing, of comfort and support and nurturing that is spread out over all the world.

Pam   That is beautiful. Your mom always says things I've never heard before.

Mom   You're doing fine but don't worry so much because that taints the message. It's like squeezing a hose. Don't try to be perfect, just be your perfect self. It's absolutely your voice that is coming through with my energy connecting with yours and it's meaningful, and again, remember, you are speaking for the human race.

Pam   I asked her, "What are you speaking for, Betty?"

Mom   We're speaking for the angelic realm, the spirit guides, all that is, the higher realms. We are doing our best to translate it into human understanding and words, even if it is a minimal or a smaller version of the grandness of it, but it still all matters. It is the intention of the message that matters. Get really clear on your intention of what you want people to hear and feel and sense, more than the exact descriptions. Everyone that reads this book is going to come from a different understanding and teaching of heritage and history. They will hear this message differently too. We can't be expected to talk to everyone. The filter is to just be yourself. Bottom line—let go, let loose, be yourself.

Pam   By the way, she's congratulating you.

Mom   Many times, you have started to put a little bit of filter on your words when you start worrying about the message, trying to make it fit, like Cinderella with the shoe.

Pam   This is funny, Jane.

Mom   Go barefoot. Stop trying to squeeze it into a certain format. You do not need restrictions. Just be free with the energy and free with the words.

Jane   I like being barefoot. I do start to worry about how this book will be received. I need to let it go. I do have a question about the format of our book. So far, I have Part One, Part Two, and Part Three. Does this feel right?

Mom   There's going to be a Part Four. Also, a Prologue and an Epilogue.

Pam   She also wants me to remind you that you don't need me to translate these messages.

Mom   You have prepared your heart. I can feel that you are now wide open to communicate and receive this conversation directly between us. You're doing good. Have faith on a big scale. You must know that you're in service and that you are showing up and being present while doing your very best. Your integrity and faith will guide you to the important, valuable, and helpful information. So please allow yourself to expand to Soul Families and Light Beings now and in other lifetimes.

CHAPTER THIRTY-TWO

PLACED IN YOUR HEART

I am filled with heart-racing fear and raging doubt again this morning. I reach for my laptop anyway. Thoughts are swirling around in my head like ants at a summer picnic. The old familiar feeling of disbelief in my abilities and the dread drubbing away in my gut grabs me by the throat. Even though these noisy thoughts loom large, I inhale deeply and exhale to release them. Faith, trust, and intent enter in, replacing the negative clamor.

I am a spiritually strong woman communicating daily with my mother, who just happens to be on the other side. I not only believe but also know that the conversation I am having with her is happening in real time. Her remains may be buried in a small cemetery in Gaylord, Michigan, but her spirit is alive and available to me as she continues to evolve, learn, and grow in The Next Room.

Regardless of the fabricated noise that dances a jig through my head, I am writing our story to the best of my abilities. I know her unearthly messages and graceful guidance is not only essential for me to hear, but they are also meant to be shared. I am fortified with courage as I reflect on what she recently articulated through Pam.

This book will not be for everyone Jane, and that's okay. Not everyone is ready to receive what we have to say. Those that need to hear our message will find it. Please just write what has been placed in your heart.

PART FOUR
CONVERSATIONS WITH MOM

PART FOUR PRAYER

Dear Divine Energy of All,

I open up my arms, tilt my head back, and open up my heart to the heavens in wonder of receiving the desired intention of moving our story forward with truth and grace.

I lay down my ego before you and suspend all judgement. May I release the need for likes, comments, attention, ratings, and the trappings of praise.

Shine your light and pure love. Illuminate my path so that I am open and aware while receiving these words of enlightenment.

I pray for my purpose to be aligned for the greater good of all humankind, as I stay rooted in my integrity while allowing my spirit to soar.

I am surrounded in gratitude.

Amen.

CHAPTER THIRTY-THREE

Ask and It Shall Be Given to You

As I prayed this morning, my thoughts kept circling back toward divine order. Instantly, I sensed the familiar tinge of Spirit. My heart opens up to welcome this warm sensation. It is an astonishing rush of energy that engulfs my senses. As the enchanting tingle arrives and flows through me, it leaves behind in its wake feelings of harmony, reverence, and present-mind awareness.

This connection to Source takes place while I am sitting in my cozy little studio. My husband built it for me as a recording studio. It serves a dual purpose now. I record my podcast and occasional commercials for companies and businesses, but most of the time I sit in here and write. It's a private and engaging space tucked into a corner of our garage. On my large sturdy glass-top table sits my desktop computer. It is playing my essential writing soundtrack by Ludovico Einaudi softly in the background. His music is transcendent and can invoke great emotion in me.

The epiphany that my mother just shared with me, that our story will have a Part Four, took me by surprise. Even though this idea frightens me, it thrills me at the same time.

I start to meditate on how to connect with my mother, without the metaphysical assistance of my psychic friend, Pam. While I am doing so, a line from a Bible verse from Matthew pops in my head: "Ask and it shall be given to you."

So, in the privacy of my studio, with a lighted candle, my favorite picture of Mom and me on the beach, and my puppy curled up alongside my bare feet, I begin to ask my mother questions. She responds with such vivid clarity that my fingers cannot type fast enough to keep up with her.

My mother is my co-author, and it is with her tender guidance that I can shine light upon the magnitude of the Divine Love that awaits each of us in The Next Room.

CHAPTER THIRTY-FOUR

THE CONVERSATION BEGINS

I'm listening, Mom. What is it that you would like me to know?

You are never alone, you can't possibly get it wrong, and never forget that grace and glory are your divine birthright.

What do you mean when you say you are never alone?

When you are born, there are many individuals cheering you on who have decided to help you along on your life's journey. Some of them you will know and recognize as family members or friends. Many of them you have never met on your side, but the moment you transition to The Next Room you'll recognize their essence, their spirit, and their energy.

Did we work this out in a previous lifetime?

Yes, this is your tribe. You worked it out with them in The Next Room before you were born. They are with you, always. Sometimes, they catch you as you fall. Many times, they sit with you as you weep in despair, doing nothing more than just being there beside you, helping you absorb your pain.

What do you mean that you can't possibly get it wrong?

It is your life experience. It is all designed by the Divine Energy of All and you cannot possibly get it wrong.

What about mistakes I've made along the way?

We like to call them lessons, Jane. Mistakes are when you inadvertently put salt in a recipe that calls for sugar.

What about these lessons? How do I recognize them and avoid repeating them?

You obviously know what these lessons are, or you would not be asking me this question.

Is this forgiveness?

There really is nothing to forgive. As we talked about with Pam earlier, even the word states that it is For Giving.

But I want to be better, do better, grow and learn.

Isn't that precisely what you are doing right now?

Good point.

Thank you. I am trying to break this down as simply and straightforwardly as possible. It's not that I think you won't be able to grasp the concepts, it's just easier for me to speak from my heart to yours and give you the most direct answer. I know you enjoy this type of communication.

I do. Thanks, Mom.

You're welcome, sweetheart. I miss you, too.

How did you know I was missing you, right at that moment?

I see you, Jane. I'm sitting right here with you now in your cozy studio. I see you typing away on your computer with your puppy at your feet. I know you have your treasured picture of us at the beach in a frame on your desk. I hear your favorite writing music playing in the background. I see the tears in your eyes. I'm with you always.

I love that you are here with me. I truly feel you in each thought.

That is because I have never left you. I only let go of the physical side of my life. My true essence is still very much alive. Although, I have grown.

What do you mean by that?

I've become a wiser form of energy. I have expanded to include more of everything. I see more love, more beauty, more compassion, more peace, more understanding. It's an exponential growth. It's beyond any scope of what I felt to be true when I was in human form as your mother. I had no idea that it would be like this. It is so vast, so big, and so enormously beautiful.

Wow, that's a wonderful depiction of your growth. I love that your expansion has been so fulfilling.

More than words could ever properly express.

So, each soul has a completely different experience when they cross?

Absolutely, just like your here and now. No two souls can experience the same thing. We are all constantly evolving to a higher level of consciousness. We each have a unique and rare experience, exclusive to each individual.

I am so grateful that you are happy with the direction of our book. You've really helped me along the way. I am so sorry it's taken so long for me to actually get moving on this.

Please don't apologize. You were not ready. I felt your anguish and I experienced your pain and deep grief along with you. I kept watch over all of you. It's so gratifying to know and to feel how deeply I was loved. I felt it from each and every one of my children, as well as your dad, and all of my magnificent grandchildren. I was a very blessed woman, and I had an incredible life with all of you.

We really were a great family, weren't we, Mom?

Yes, but I would like to change that to we are a great family.

Another astute point. Even though you must have seen the wheels come off after you left.

I did not see that as wheels coming off. I feel it was all necessary growth for each of you. You see, we adjust. With each loss, each moment of sadness, each time we grieve—we grow.

All very important facets on our individual journey during our life experience.

That's a good way to put it.

I like to think so. Each of us has a particular life experience. There is no possibility for any two people to truly understand each other's chosen path. That is why it's so important to stay on your own course.

So, allowing?

Yes, allowing the other person to expand and grow at the rate that they have chosen. Everyone is different. Allow the difference. It's so much more peaceful to let people flow in their own way.

You know I was really freaked out when you suggested a Part Four. I honestly did not know how I would be able to do this without the Pam's assistance.

You not only can, but you are. It's me. I am here with you right now. I know that you know this to be true. I know you can feel my guidance, my words, my energy and direction.

I am so loving this right now. I'm actually feeling really blessed and fortunate that you are taking the time to write this book with me.

There is no such thing as time. I feel your desire, that's all. I know that in terms of your earthly space that you have wanted to do this for a very long while. You just needed to trust in yourself. I knew you could do this. We could do this. You just needed to get quiet, listen, and have faith.

Ha! Is that a dig at my ability to talk?

Not at all. I love listening to you, especially when you make up songs and sing. What I mean by quiet is to truly turn inside yourself. You know—that tender space, where only God can touch. It's such a beautiful, exclusive space. God speaks to us through our hearts.

Isn't this what you and I are doing?

Well, first of all, I am not God but rather a piece of the Almighty Energy of All. We all are. You know the Bible phrase, "God is love?" As simple as it is, it's the closest thing that I have found to be the truth.

We really are all connected, aren't we?

Absolutely. That's why when you hurt another you really are only hurting yourself.

Please explain.

Think of your connection to this Almighty Divine Love, or God, as being delicate pieces of thread that are woven together with billions upon billions of other delicate pieces of thread to produce a universal blanket of love. This blanket not only covers the universe you know, but the thousands of universes that exist that you do not know. This thread of love blankets over all of them.

So, I shouldn't pull on someone else's thread?

Well, you may, and many times do. The result is always the same. You end up causing yourself pain.

This helps me a lot.

I'm glad. It's all an inner knowledge that everyone already knows. I think, perhaps, we just forget it when we are in human form.

When you cross and let go of your body and return to source, do you remember all of this information?

Yes, immediately. However, I like to think of it as wisdom instead of information. Anyone can gather information. Wisdom is felt on what you may refer to as a deeper spiritual level.

Another aha moment for me.

I'm so happy I can help shed light on your thoughts.

You always felt wise to me when you were here with me as my mom.

For clarification, I am still your mom. I appreciate you saying that. I used the gifts God gave me to the best of my ability, but I had much to learn.

I'm so happy you are still my mom. Are you learning now?

So much. We covered many of the lessons through Pam in Part Three. Is there something specific we did not cover that you would like to know?

I have many questions.

Ask away. That's why I am here. First of all, let me say that I am so happy you are opening up to allow this stream of consciousness. I knew you had it in you. I knew you needed to get out of your own way and stop doubting your ability to receive these expressions of grace. I know how important it is for you to be taken seriously, but does it truly matter? In the long run, your truth is all that you have. There is not another soul on your planet or beyond who knows what you know. So, if you are worried about what someone else will think, let that worry evaporate. It will only stop you from living your grander purpose.

So, I should stop resisting and worrying about whether I am getting this right?

You are getting it right. It's our truth. How can anyone really doubt our story of our truth? This book may not be for everyone and that's okay.

Okay, message received. Tell me about Jesus.

I like to say that he is perfection in a being. His energy is as selfless and pure as it comes. He truly taught so much in his 33 years on the planet and he continues to teach now. I love that you love him so much. He is a divine soul. He has so much goodness, grace, and generosity. He doesn't blame anyone for what happened to him. He understands that it was just part of his story.

Why are we not getting his legacy straight?

What exactly do you mean?

I guess what I want to know is, if you are a believer in Christ and his teachings and you profess your love for him and his ways, how can you still blatantly lie, cheat or harm another human being?

What you must understand is that free will is a gift that we were given from the beginning of time. If someone chooses to follow Christ but not act in a Christ-like manner, this is also their choice. We honestly do not condemn or shame them into doing anything differently. They will return to Source soon enough and see the truth again. It's all part of their journey. It is not your position in life to try to correct, change, or point out their differences. Your passage is as individual to you as theirs is to them. Please allow others the respect, dignity and opportunity to do as they wish.

Grace and glory are my divine birthright? Please explain.

I am happy to. What is important to realize is that each and every soul on planet Earth is filled with grace and they are each part of the good Lord's glory, every single one of us. We are all pieces of God's greater good. No one soul is above another. We are all born equal in the divine eyes of God.

What about privilege?

Again, this is free will in its finest form. It may be hard to conceptualize but we all have a hand in our story. When we enter, we choose when we are born, where and what type of life we lead.

How do we not remember this?

Some of us actually do. Many do not. It protects us on our quest if we do not remember exactly what we decided before we were born.

So, déjà vu. Is that an old memory?

Yes. Maybe not in its purest form but it is a feeling of knowing someone, somewhere, or an experience from before.

What about the Holy Spirit tingle or goosebumps as many refer to this feeling?

This is quite simply your knowing.

I have this happen quite frequently.

Yes, I know.

Is this you reaching out?

Many times, yes. It's not always me. You have a host of other spirits that are committed to your transformative expansion. They reach out to you with this sensation when you are on track. This feeling helps you to recognize when you are in the right space of growth.

I love this feeling.

It's fun, isn't it? It's sort of a nice little sensory guide.

What about when I have the feeling that it is a certain soul that is delivering this message to me?

When this happens and you blurt out the name of a soul, it's really a moment of pure gratitude. Your family and friends who have traveled this path before you love it when you acknowledge them.

How do I know for sure if it's the person I think it is?

Good question. Quite simply put, it is exactly who you think it is.

I love to talk to people that have gone before me.

We know you do. I want you to know how much it is appreciated. When you call out to us, we feel that we are in service. It's part of our on-going growth as ever-expanding souls.

I stopped worrying about what people would say regarding my conversations with dead people.

We prefer the word transitioned.

Thank you.

You're welcome, sweetheart. What else would you like to talk about today?

I love when you call me that name.

Sweetheart?

Yes.

Why wouldn't I refer to you by all of our old familiar names? It helps you to hear me if I speak to you as your mother, not as a stranger.

I'd like to ask you about difficult relationships and conflicts.

First off, they are difficult only if you wish them so.

What do you mean by that?

Exactly what I said. If you feel and speak about these relationships and people as difficult, then that is exactly what they will become in your life. And, if you refer to them as easy, that is what they become.

What if they are family members?

Wayne Dyer said it best: "If you change the way you look at things, the things you look at change."

I love that quote.

It's true. Our perception is our reality. However, you can shift your perception at any time. Our brains are powerful. You need only to change your view to see things from a completely different perspective. It's much like when I was describing looking through a hole in a box. You only see what's in the box until you step away from that box and pull back. You then see a much bigger picture.

Let's talk about working through difficult situations.

I know this has really been bothering you. Remember, I can feel your thoughts and frustration when things are not going the way you think they should go. That's the ideal time to step away, pull back, and look at the situation in a different light. Remember Jane, it's not all about you. The best advice

127

I can give you or anyone else going through conflict is to let go of it. In simple terms that I have heard you repeat over and over—let go, let God.

Okay, I got it. I actually know this to be true. It's just hard to do sometimes.

The fact that you even care enough to bring it up shows progress on this issue. You'll get there. It's all about allowing the light in. Darkness is easier sometimes. It takes effort to be angry, to point fingers, to place blame. You may gain temporary comfort, but it's actually creating inner conflict. Your soul knows the way to peace and the only way out of the darkness is through the light.

Oh Mom, that's good. Is it possible to continue to learn and grow while we are here?

Of course. Why wouldn't you continue to grow and learn?

Well, it's just that I see so many obvious lessons being repeated.

Yours, or those of others?

Both.

Stop that. I'm serious. If a lesson comes to you and you know deep within your being that it is a lesson, get it and move on. I do not mean to sound trite, but honestly, you know when you are in the wrong. Conversely, you know on a deep, cellular level when you are receiving signals that feel right.

Yes. I do.

I know you do. It's incredibly important that you breathe into this space of knowing. It's a treasure. Truly, a buried treasure of yours and one of your greatest gifts. Dig it up and allow it to wash over you so you can move forward in learning what it is you need to know. Then move on to the next lesson.

Let's stop for today. I'm slightly overwhelmed.

Be whelmed, Jane. It's a much better space to dwell.

Okay, Mom, thank you for being here today. I love you more than words can express.

I know you do, honey. I feel your deep admiration and love for me. It is my honor to have been your mother in this lifetime.

Wait. You were you not always my mother?

You need to rest. We'll tackle this tomorrow.

CHAPTER THIRTY-FIVE

My Mother's Mother

It's a new day, a new dawn. I had a great night's sleep, and I woke up thinking about you, about us, and about our book.

That is completely understandable. "It's like a song I can hear playing right in my ear, but I can't sing, I can't help listening."

Did you just quote a lyric from one of my favorite songs?

Yes, I like that song too.

I didn't know you knew about Jackson Browne.

Like I told you before, I'm learning. And of course, I have heard you play that song over and over. Jackson has a rather good grasp on the obvious.

That makes me laugh. Let's move on. I want to go back to the thought that you were my mother in this lifetime, but you have not *always* been my mother. Is this correct?

Yes.

What have we been to one another?

Love. We have been pure loving souls that have decided to travel together this lifetime and beyond. We made this decision long ago. It was eons, actually.

Is this why I have always felt so protective of you?

Yes.

Is it possible our roles were reversed in another lifetime and I was your mother?

Yes, you were.

Was I good mother?

Yes, the best. You were hard working, dedicated, strict but incredibly fair.

To be honest with you, this makes total sense to me. It also aligns with what another psychic medium told me years ago. She said that the reason I always felt the need to take care of you and be with you is that I felt a deep level of protection for you—a protection that only a mother feels for her child. She said it's because I was your mother in a past life. This thought gave me such great understanding and peace, as strange as it may sound.

Why do you feel this sounds strange?

It's also not the easiest conversation to have with someone and explain that you were your mother's mother in a past life.

Then don't.

Don't what?

Explain. It's not your position to explain anything to anyone. Just be you. If someone needs to hear what you have to say, they will find you and listen. Nothing is accomplished by applying effort. That is another thing you can let go. That doesn't mean you cannot explore and talk about deeper thoughts, like what's beyond your here and now and even your past. Keep exploring, but for the love of all things holy, stop trying to illuminate others that are not ready to hear what you have to say.

Okay, I got it. But if I don't talk about what I'm doing, how will they find our book?

The beauty of a fathomless connection is the miraculous wonder of all pieces fitting together exactly where they need to fit. You seriously do not need to force any of this life experience, just allow it to happen and let go of the outcome. You must also remember to stop and consciously breathe. I cannot stress this one simple, physical expression of life enough. Just breathe and trust. The right people have already found you and you know this to be true, yes?

Yes, I do. I have many charismatic, fascinating friends.

You have attracted a considerable array of curious souls that are here on a soul grouping mission to expand the conscious thought on the planet.

I know. I'm always amazed at the conversations I have, and I seem to be attracting even more of these intriguing people daily.

You are, because you are compellingly open to receiving these connections.

Let's discuss past lives. Have I had others?

Yes, you have had numerous.

So, in essence, we just keep going?

Yes, we do. We keep going and growing, although not all souls decide to come back into rotation. Many are quite cozy and satisfied to stay right where they are.

So, we have a choice?

Yes, free will, remember? It exists on every level of our souls' experience.

So, there is no judgment?

Oh, gosh no. What's to judge? All souls are ever evolving at a pace that is comfortable for that soul.

I'm curious. Why would someone choose a life of poverty or pain?

Simply put, to help humanity move forward. Perhaps it is not viewed as poverty or pain, but simply an opportunity to expand a boundary of growth.

Okay, I'm satisfied. Except, I need to know. Have you returned?

Do you mean right now?

Yes.

I have. My energy is actually already in several other incarnations on the planet.

That's wild. Do I know these people?

No, you do not.

So, let me get this straight. You are in The Next Room as my mother and speaking to me now and you have already incarnated in other forms?

Yes. Is this hard for you to understand?

Well, frankly, yes. I guess I didn't give a lot of thought to the fact that our energy could split off into multiple directions.

We don't split, so to speak. It's my energy as whole as it is in this moment. I'll let you sit with that thought for a moment.

This gives me a lot to ponder. Let's talk about prayer.

What would you like to know?

Does prayer help?

Without a shadow of a doubt, prayer helps. Let me explain. Prayer is a resuscitation of pleasing words bringing in the Almighty Divine Energy of All, God. When you incite a mantra, a devotion, or a plea of help, you are opening to this energy in the purest form of worship.

So, in essence, when we pray, we are speaking directly to God?

Yes. Think of prayer as a verbal love letter. Who doesn't love receiving a well-formed and refined letter of adoration? It not only lifts our spirits, but it raises our vibration to match the affection of love that God bestows upon us. Your prayers are love letters to God.

What if the prayer is more like a plea? Like when you were in the hospital. I was not exactly reciting a verbal love letter to God. I was actually rather rude and demanding.

Jane, God does not hold your humanness against you. The Divine created you, demands and all.

Thank God, literally.

That's funny.

Let's talk about raising our vibration.

This is such an important thing to note. Please write this one down.

Ha! Is that a nod to Abraham-Hicks?

Yes, I knew you would appreciate that. Okay, in all seriousness, raising our vibration to how we want to feel is essential. I know you're aware of how horrible you feel when you're angry or upset and, conversely, how buoyant and joyous you feel when you are happy.

Yes, I do. It upsets me when I allow myself to react and be foolish over silly things that I clearly have no control over. I have actually watched myself go from one extreme to the other quickly and it's not pleasant.

I know. I have seen you. I also know that you have grown in leaps and bounds since I was here as your mom. When you are irrational, your brain chemistry changes. More adrenaline is released, and you easily can spin out of control. When you are in a space of feeling good, happy hormones arrive, like dopamine, serotonin, and endorphins. Getting a handle on your emotional state is not always easy, but it is possible to flip a switch to feeling better with simple things like breathing, exercise, laughter, music, or simply sitting still and observing nature.

What about chemical imbalances?

I am not a doctor, even though your dad liked to tease me about being one. Real imbalance in the brain is something that only a clinical doctor should deal with. So many times, people suffer in silence due to the stigma attached to mental illness. It takes a brave and courageous soul to step forth and seek help.

Okay, I'm pooped. We've been at this all day. I'm open to a visit with you in my dreams. I always love seeing you. Please feel free to swing by anytime.

I visit you more than you remember. I'll make a point of stopping by tonight. Please give my love to your family. You really have a fabulous gang of four.

You mean five?

Of course, your new little puppy. I've got Honey, by the way. You'll see her again. She really liked you as her mom. She's a beautiful soul.

I miss her, but Mamba certainly has filled a void.

Yes, she has. She's rather brilliant, as well as a beauty.

Thanks, Mom, I really love her. Hopefully I will see you tonight and we'll catch up tomorrow.

Sweet dreams, my baby girl.

CHAPTER THIRTY-SIX

"Whatever You Focus on Expands"

Good morning. If you did visit me, I don't remember. I kept waking up thinking about you as I was willing myself to have a dream with you in it.

I was there. You are trying too hard to see me. You see, Jane, when we are in a relaxed state of sleep, we allow ourselves to travel to a deeper space in our subconsciousness. We can time-travel, fly, rescue a cat, breath underwater, communicate with animals, visit with transitioned souls, and even leave the house without clothes on. You need only to relax and stop trying so hard to see me. I am with you now. You must know the best gift we can give one another is to be present for our book.

I do. It's just that after I see you in a dream, I wake up feeling so happy and fulfilled. I savor it all day and really try to remember every detail. Like the last dream I had with you, you had on a red polka-dot dress. It was so unlike you to wear something like that.

I did that so you would remember. It worked, yes?

Yes.

Okay, so what would you like to talk about today? I know you had several thoughts when you were walking your puppy this morning. Let's start there.

You sure know how to make things easy on a gal. Okay, what I want to talk to you about is the art of gratitude and giving thanks.

I love this topic. When you are thankful for everything in your life, your awareness grows. Even the not-so-pleasant parts of life are designed for your benefit. They require you to view them from a different angle to allow the gratitude to flow.

How can we be expected to give thanks for things that are painful and unpleasant?

You're not.

Please expand.

You are never "expected" to give thanks. Learning how to be in a constant state of gratitude takes practice. It's a stunning lesson of growth when you can look around you and say thank you— for everything.

What about whatever you focus on expands? If I'm giving thanks for something unpleasant, won't I receive more of that unpleasantness?

No, you're looking at it wrong. Gratitude is living in a state of grace. When you can say thank you, it's not important to focus on the negative side of whatever it is. Just give thanks for the lesson, the long game, so to speak. Many times, things may occur that appear tragic in the moment, but ultimately are not that at all. It's just life. It's a ride with ups and downs. This life experience never ends. It's the in-between times that are the magic. You might as well give thanks for all of it now. Giving thanks will also raise your vibration.

A perfect segue.

Raising your vibration is key. We are all just particles of energy. When we vibrate love, we'll attract more love.

Conversely, if you are vibrating hate, your vibration is super low, and you will create more of a negative flow to you. Envision a super-strong magnet. Manifest yours to be one of gratitude, love, laughter, fun, peace, abundance, and understanding. You will literally attract these things into your life because you are a vibrational match. I'm sure you must know someone who is always complaining.

Yes.

No matter what it is that they are experiencing, even if it's something good, they may feel more comfortable in the space of the downside and seek out this feeling. This really is wasted energy. Do your best to limit your time around this type of negativity. Like attracts like, and as I've heard you say many times— life is short, but it is wide. Spend your time in the space in the wideness of life. This is where the joy is found.

I like the ideas of being whelmed and the wideness of life. Thank you.

You're welcome, honey. What's next?

Well, I'd really like to ask you about connecting with other souls that have traveled before me, but my brain is sort of scattered right now.

How about we break for now? We'll start here tomorrow morning.

That sounds great. I love you, Mom. My heart is overflowing with gratitude for you and your willingness to share with me right now in this moment in time.

You have no idea. The pleasure is all mine. It feels good to be able to connect with you on such a deep spiritual level. I love you, too. Good night, sweetheart.

CHAPTER THIRTY-SEVEN

SIGNS, DIMES, AND THE THINGS WE LEAVE BEHIND

O kay, I'm back and ready to roll. Please tell me about the souls that are on the other side with you.

There are numerous souls that you know about and many you have never met on that side but will remember them again when you cross. That will be a while from now, by the way.

Do you mean I'm going to be on this side for a while?

Yes, although time means nothing. Enjoy every sandwich.

Another great reference to music. I love Warren Zevon. That message from you is good to hear. I feel healthy and I am happy. I want to accomplish so much more (besides writing this book). I'm praying for grandchildren when the timing is right, and you know about my passion for travel.

You will have both. Grands and grand travel.

This makes me incredibly happy to hear. Even though I know deep down that both of those things are true.

They are. You really didn't need to confirm either of those things with me, did you?

No, I guess I didn't. Let's move on to signs.

Excellent topic. I love sending them. Although not everyone is as skilled at seeing them, feeling them, or picking up on them as I would like. It still doesn't stop me from sending them.

So, the dimes?

Yes, from me, and also your Grandpa Harmon. He's such a tender old soul. He really felt bad leaving you when you were so little. He really enjoyed giving you a ride on his foot. Even though you were so young, you have that memory seared into your memory bank, yes?

I do. I think of him often and because Uncle Earl looked so much like him, I felt like I transferred my affection over to him as though Grandpa actually never left.

The Harmons are a good lot.

Yes, they are. You must feel how much you were beloved in the family and what an important role you played.

I do. But honestly, no more special than every other member of the Harmon family. Each of us has it in us to leave a legacy of goodness behind in our wake. It's really an individual choice while we are here in human form to decide what our legacy will be.

I love hearing that. The gifts we leave behind, yes?

Yes, there are generations upon generations of ideas, dreams, passions, recipes, love letters, and family traits. It's fascinating to see it from this perspective, as you will someday. There are really no words to describe the magnitude of this expansiveness. It will be something that you literally plug back into and feel—rather than see.

So, back to the dimes?

Simple, really. I knew that when you were a little girl you would always stop to pick up a penny, so I thought by leaving you dimes I would really grab your attention.

What's wild is that Betty, Thomas, and Tom started finding them too.

Yes, I know. It was really fun to see the excitement on each of your faces when they would find one. It is a super fun game that we have had with your family. It's easy to play with all of you because you believe.

We believe?

Yes, in the afterlife, the signs, the deep divine mystery of it all. It doesn't frighten you or your family. All four of you are curious and believers that you can and do connect with those of us on the other side.

What are some of the other signs you use?

Well, I blow bubbles and send balloons to other family members. I have whispered tenderly in several ears to let them know I have never left their side. Sometimes I arrive as a vivid dream, or I will send wildlife through nature. Many times, it is difficult for individuals to receive these signs because their pain and anguish overwhelms them from what is right in front of them. In essence, they choose not to believe that it is a sign from me or another loved one.

How do we know that these signs are from the person we are thinking of?

Great question. If a person pops into your thoughts at the exact moment you find a dime, or see a random balloon floating in the air, or perhaps a duck swimming in a pond, you will know it is them.

Is there a way we can ask for a sign?

Yes, and many do, frequently. We hear you. However, winning the lottery is not a sign that those on the other side wish to perform.

What are other ways that our loved ones in The Next Room connect?

You are asking a question you already have the answer to, but for the sake of our book I'll indulge you. We reach out through each moment. We send you gifts of feathers and dancing butterflies, cardinals and fat robins in the springtime, and hummingbirds that zoom up to your face to say hello. Electronics are another favorite. A song that you hear in the exact moment you were thinking of that person—this is your loved one. There's honestly no limit to the ways you can connect to the other realm. It's as simple as knowing you can connect with them and then allowing them the pleasure of doing so.

It reminds me of the beautiful poem by Henry Scott-Holland, *Death is Nothing at All*. I wonder if I need to get permission to print that piece in this book.

Yes, you do, and I think it would be a lovely addition.

"Death is nothing at all. It does not count. I have only slipped away into the next room. Nothing has happened. Everything remains exactly as it was. I am I, and you are you, and the old life that we lived so fondly together is untouched, unchanged. Whatever we were to each other, that we are still. Call me by the old familiar name. Speak of me in the easy way which you always used. Put no difference into your tone. Wear no forced air of solemnity or sorrow. Laugh as we always laughed at the little jokes that we enjoyed together. Play, smile, think of me, pray for me. Let my name be ever the household word that it always was. Let it be spoken without an effort, without the ghost of a shadow upon it. Life means all that it ever meant. It is the same as it ever was. There is absolute and unbroken continuity. What is this death but a negligible accident? Why should I be out of mind because I am out of sight? I am but waiting for you, for an interval, some-where very near, just round the corner. All is well. Nothing is hurt; nothing is lost. One brief moment and all will be as it was before. How we shall laugh at the trouble of parting when we meet again!"

—Henry Scott Holland, *Death is Nothing at All*

What do you recommend we do each day to become more aware?

Meditate, or if that is not something you are comfortable with or knowledgeable about doing, just sit quietly and focus on breathing deliberately. Open your hands palm up in your lap to receive this divine invitation. Envision God beaming love directly to you, through you, around you, shooting up from your feet, flowing down through the top of your head and swirling around your heart. Ask God to be with you always. Ask him to walk with you, drive with you, sing, dance, cook, and communicate with you. God is always with us but the invitation to allow him to be one with us is a powerful practice. That's why prayer usually starts with a version of Dear God, Heavenly Father, Almighty, Beloved, Creator, In the name of Jesus—or even, Divine Energy of All. Prayer is when we talk to God. Meditation is when God speaks to us.

What about my version of God versus someone else's version?

There are literally billions of interpretations of this Almighty Energy of All and there is simply no way to get it wrong. And not one way to get it right, as right and wrong are just human terms. God is in you. He's there no matter if you pray without ceasing or once in a lifetime, God is okay with all levels of worship. God's energy is forever flowing and growing and available to us always in all ways. Simply put, Jane, God is All.

I love this interpretation of the Almighty Energy of All. I'm continually amazed at how I grow in my acceptance and belief of this generosity of grace and goodness.

It's really something, isn't it? To be in a space of constant awareness of this divine love is really the essence of humanity. It's empowering to watch the growth of individuals that you have grouped together during this lifetime.

So, you obviously can see when we are stretching and reaching for a better elevated perspective?

Yes. Think about it like a huge stadium packed full of loving souls cheering you along on your life's journey. They are all sitting on the edge of their seats in anticipation of you to grow in your faith. They want you to grasp for higher understanding. They encourage you to help someone up that has fallen down. They can see you gaze toward the stars in awe and know you are in a state of wonder. They smile as you delicately touch a flower or pet your puppy.

What if someone doesn't buy into a higher power and literally shuns these ideas and thoughts?

We don't feel it is possible. Perhaps this is their persona here and now and they have adopted this protective layer and exterior to keep these thoughts at bay. However, when they are in a dream state or feeling happiness, petting a little kitten or admiring a huge tree or watching a dragonfly flit across the backyard, they know it, deep inside them where God lives. Maybe they are not allowing themselves to speak it, but they feel it.

So, God doesn't give up on non-believers?

Goodness, no! God is Almighty and everywhere so there is nothing to give up on. We are all God's children made in his likeness. We are all parts of the greater whole. To give up on even the tiniest piece of humanity is not possible.

That's good to hear. I'm actually rather fascinated by atheists and agnostics.

Yes, I know. We love that you treat them no differently than your spiritually elevated friends. They have brilliant thoughts as well. They just choose to not trust the "organized" part of what has happened to faith. They also made a conscious choice for this path of non-believing so they can enlighten and move the narrative forward in the way they feel is most helpful. We all have free will to honor a higher power of our own understanding. No matter what this higher power represents, it is ours and ours alone. We are all particles of energy which can change forms but will never disappear. Our energy will one day transform whether we believe this to be true or not.

Is this one of the lessons you are learning about?

Yes, and so many more.

Let's talk about the existence of God again for clarification of the numerous differences between all of the various religions on the planet.

I love this topic. As we spoke before, God is all. Therefore, each religion, no matter what they are called or the traditions they chose to perform in the name of their idea of God, all boil down to the very same thought about this Divine Energy of All. That is, this Supreme Being—is Love.

So, in essence, there are many doors to The Next Room?

Yes, so very many. We all belong to the greater good and the energy of all. We are all brothers and sisters born of the same light and love. When we send thoughts of love or project our loving energy out from our bodies into the universe, it is received. It has a powerful effect on everything around us when we tap into this greater source. This energy will bring about vibrations of feeling good within our own body. You see Jane, when you love something that you physically cannot see, whether it is a person, place, idea, animal, country or other planet, you are vibrating in a belief mode of pure love.

Okay, another pivot. Why is it that I procrastinate something that I feel in my heart is so important?

Do you mean this book?

Yes.

Believe it or not, you started writing this shortly after I left. The pure fact that you have volumes of journals packed full of stories, ideas, events, and poems is what you were meant to do. All of this is our book.

I know, Mom. Why was it so hard to actually get started?

You're a silly goose. You did get "started," as you like to say. This moment right here, right now is all that truly matters. Do you not get this?

I do. I guess I like to beat up on myself for not doing it sooner

Sooner than what? Again, this moment. Right here is all that matters.

So, be here now?

Yes, another great song.

I'm so happy you are enjoying my music.

I do. You have great taste, it's very eclectic.

So, here we are. Just you and me in my studio in San Diego communicating with one another. Isn't it wild?

No, it is absolutely not wild. It's perfectly perfect. Although perfection is something only achieved by the highest, Divine Energy of All—God.

On my walk this morning I was thinking about potential.

It is limitless. There is not one thing that you could not achieve if you decided to make it so. The only reason you may not reach a certain goal is that you yourself do not believe that that goal is attainable. Many times, individuals stop themselves before they've begun simply by the words they choose to speak.

Words are important.

Yes, so very important. I know you've heard that the universe is somewhat like a big ear. When you say something, the Universe responds by putting forth the thing that you continuously think about. It doesn't discern between good or bad. It just hears you talking about something over and over and figures this is what you want.

This brings up another question. What's the difference between God and the Universe?

God is All. The universe is the container that holds all of the magic that God designed, which is everything that you are currently experiencing.

So, when you say the universe hears everything, does that mean God?

What I mean by that is the energy that is in your life experience in this time-space continuum, the complete universe that you can see, travel, experience and feel. This universal energy is a living breathing entity that responds to your thoughts, ideas, words and desires. God is the energy of love that is all. God is the universe and all the love contained herein.

Okay, let's cover a few topics that are important to me. How do you feel about acceptance versus tolerance?

This one is easy. Tolerance is a term that could be disposed of. To be tolerant means you are "putting up with" the person, place, situation. Acceptance is the art of allowing the person, place, situation to be exactly as it is presented to you. I'm afraid we have become a rather intolerant society.

How do you feel about kindness?

There's never enough. Kindness can be expressed in a myriad of ways. Kindness is a gentle touch, loving words, or even making someone a sandwich. It's incredibly important to work at being kind every single day, even when you're annoyed. Stop, breathe, and think to yourself, "How can I do this task with loving kindness?"

This next topic is near and dear to my heart. What wisdom do you have for me about people that need assistance, whether they are homeless or just down on their luck?

Help them, always.

Please go on.

If you have, give. If someone is hungry, feed them. If you see someone without shoes, take yours off and give them to them. Help them always, Jane. It's one of your greatest gifts.

Generosity?

Yes, you were born with a rather substantial generous bone. Never, ever let anyone stop you from giving. You were born to give. Please give daily, no matter if it's a smile, a dollar, old clothes, a casserole, flowers, or a random card with cash. There's no way on God's big beautiful planet that you can ever, ever give too much. Do you remember what your dad always used to say?

Yes. "You can't outgive the Lord."

Exactly, keeping in mind your dad had his own interpretation of this message. However, it applies to you as well, just make it your own.

I never give because I hope to benefit in some way.

I know. You do it because you know that you only give to yourself.

Exactly, I feel so overwhelmingly good when I give that I just want to give more.

Please do. Give, give, and then give some more. It's your reason for being.

I guess this is why I love mission work so much, yes?

Yes. When I was with you in the physical, I often worried, as mothers will do, about your passion to travel to faraway places to help others in need. I knew deep down this was a special gift that you had inherited from God. I knew you were put here to spread goodness, generosity, and grace all over the world. I had to pivot to accept this as your journey.

After you left, I felt that you were with me.

That's because, once I shed my earthly form, I was free to travel along with you. You felt me by your side because I was there with you every single step of the way.

I feel like most of my trips started taking form after you left.

Yes. I felt it was time to see the world through your eyes.

You said that to me many times, when you were on this side. How did you know that I would be traveling the world?

Mother's intuition. I knew that you were born to fly from a very young age. When you called me and Dad to tell us you were moving to California when you were only 22, I knew at that moment it was time to let you go.

Thank you for "getting" me. I feel as though you always saw me. You never looked through me. You really saw me as a person. You honored my strange side.

I'm going to call that your unique side.

Let's stop for today. You've given me a great many things to contemplate.

Sounds good. I love you, too.

CHAPTER THIRTY-EIGHT

2020 Challenges

Mom, I am thinking about all of the challenges we are facing on the planet today. The year 2020 was extremely difficult for numerous reasons. What are we here to learn from the COVID-19 virus, civil unrest, the election year divisiveness, and finally, from our planet being on fire?

Last year was an enormous shift. It has not always been a pleasant one, and it is causing many disagreements and fighting, even within families. The best guidance I have for you is to stay in your own lane. This is not to say that you have to ignore the issues. Quite the contrary, you need to stay informed so you can focus your energy for the good of all humankind.

Let's talk about this more in depth.

Each and every single one of you decided to come here at this exact moment in time. You knew before you came that there were going to be deep and monumental challenges facing all of you. You willingly took this on, as you wanted to be part of this great shift in consciousness. No matter which side you fall on, your opinions are yours alone. I know how deeply you have been bothered by many of these issues. The ability to stay in a peaceful space requires super-human strength. Peace, above all, is where you need to be to help transition your life forward.

One of my favorite songs is, *Peace, Love and Understanding.* And it's the name of my veranda.

"What's so funny 'bout peace, love and understanding?" What many people are fighting and arguing about has nothing to do with the real issue.

What do you mean?

The real issue is inside of them. The feeling of being inadequate, self-doubting, a lack of trust in the message that the Divine is trying to send them.

Please explain further.

From now on I will refer to this energy as God. This is the term you are most familiar with. You see, Jane, God is always and forever on your side. It doesn't matter which side you may feel you are on. God loves you and every other single soul unequivocally. It does not matter if that soul is not choosing to be a good person or is making kindness a priority. God will always and forever love all.

This doesn't seem fair.

What's not fair? God is not standing in judgment of individuals on their deeds, good, bad or indifferent. God sees your heart, all hearts, even when the things in your heart may lead you to a not very kind action. God will never, ever desert anyone.

So, we are all created equal in God's likeness?

Yes, exactly. Once you leave this life with your limited understanding, you will feel the glory, the beauty and energy of non-stop love. It's so extensive that it will literally fill you up so that you will be overflowing in a liquid pool of grace. This feeling is like no other. Think of a time that you were the happiest you've ever been, maybe when Betty and Thomas were born and the moments those perfect little babies were placed in your arms. Feel the joy you felt and allow the memory to envelop you. Envision those first moments of pure motherly love and how they made you feel. Feel the love in your heart expand so that you physically feel as though your chest cavity is growing and growing. Now that you are remembering a state of bliss, imagine feeling like this but a million times grander. It is an impossible task, but you will feel this at some point. When you do, you will know the purity of God's love.

It sounds so wonderful.

It is. You do realize that you can create marvelous feelings of pure love while you're on Earth, too.

Yes, but it never seems to last.

That is because you get really good at being human. Stop being so human and enjoy being love.

That's funny, Mom.

What's so funny? Peace? Love? Or Understanding?

I see what you did right there.

Be still and breathe. Look up at the sky. Take your shoes off and feel the earth beneath your feet. Pet a cat or a dog. Say hello to your neighbors. Pray for everyone. Look people in the eye. Apologize when necessary. Release ill feelings and forgive misdeeds. Listen to inspiring music. Send a love letter. Buy someone a coffee. Just be.

Just be?

Yes, just be. When you sit quietly long enough and just be, this is where the magic happens.

Are you referring to messages from God?

Yes, everyone receives them. It's the recognizing part that they miss. It's that being human thing that gets in the way. Allow God's grace by opening your heart to receive the love. It's a never-ending source of light and love and it is flowing to you right now. I know by watching you that you are feeling it right now.

I am. It's hard to type with all the tears in my eyes.

You're doing just fine. Let those tears flow. They are tears of the knowledge that God is the supreme energy of all beings.

It's a good feeling when you finally get it that you are not in charge. Yield, allow, surrender, and know that the strongest, most efficient co-pilot has got your back nine ways to Sunday.

I love thinking about God as my co-pilot.

It's a lovely metaphor, isn't it?

Now I need to hear *Jesus, Savior Pilot Me.*

Another beautiful piece of music. I love all the old hymns. You see, Jane, music is a pure expression directed, written and orchestrated by God. Music is embedded deeply into our souls. Music has the influence to reach us where words, many times, will fail to connect.

What about someone who is born deaf?

Again, free will. They made this choice, perhaps so they could heighten all other senses and experience life in a different manner. By the way, music can also be felt, even when it is not heard.

I think about individuals with physical handicaps and I wonder about their quality of life.

Their quality of life is designed with them in mind. Everyone has a different life experience. You can't possibly fathom what is going on inside of another individual. Just do you and allow others in your path to do them. Trying to change, mold, or alter their experience is a waste of precious time.

Let's talk about change. Is it possible to truly change?

If you are referring to our soul, no. Our souls are a generous representation of who we really are. You can change patterns, habits, and your socks, but not your soul.

What about growth?

Yes, of course. We are all here to grow in awareness, love, patience, compassion, and kindness. These lessons find each of us in their own time.

What about time?

My, you are all over the map this morning. Time is something human beings designed from the moment of existence. It has grown into a guideline of sorts. What's important to note is each of you are only here in this life as it is, in this moment, for a limited amount of what you refer to as time. It's important to make these moments in your day and nights matter. I don't mean like doing monumental things, although you may choose to. I'm referring to the beauty and the awareness of breathing, or watching a sunrise or a sunset, or simply sitting in solitude in meditative prayer. Sending loving thoughts to everyone you happen to cross paths with is also time well spent. Above all, please remember—if you are present in the moment there is no such thing as wasted time.

I love that thought. Many times, I sit and get lost in prayer or, quite honestly, I'm not sure where my mind goes. I just allow it to wander.

That is actually a wonderful skill to have. You are in a state of just being when you do this. It is quite empowering and gives you energy. It is much like recharging your battery.

Isn't this why we sleep?

Sleep is a glorious use of time. This is when your consciousness floats away and you are traveling in other dimensions. If you can master this element of consciousness when you are awake, this is an extremely blissful place to be. It takes belief and practice to achieve this form of being, and meditation is key.

I would like to ask you about staying present.

Okay. What I'd like to express to you is that you just need to be. There is nothing more to do. Many times, when we were on your side in our earthly bodies, we get so busy with being human that we forget our souls' purpose.

Our souls' purpose?

Yes, each of us has a deep and meaningful purpose to fill. The trick is to allow it to come to you. You need not search high and low for it. You instinctively already know what it is. Just be and it will find you, instead of the other way around.

How do we know when we find it?

You'll feel it, Jane. It is a gentle nudge, or a God wink, as you're fond of saying.

I feel as though I have found mine.

Yes, you have. Just keep on being in your now. Honor every moment and don't wait for things to get just right before you begin. So many people wait until it's just right, and then they never really get started. It is always the right time.

Please explain.

This moment, right here, right now is the only one that matters. So, if you are waiting for this moment, it's already gone. You missed it. You'll have literally waited yourself out of the right moment.

I am in constant awe of this gift you are giving me right now.

Just keep showing up, Jane. That's all you need to do. Be one with this moment and allow the Divine Energy of All— God, to shine her light.

Her light?

Yes, her light, his light, ALL light. God is ubiquitous. So much bigger and grander than any gender form.

CHAPTER THIRTY-NINE

Doubting Jane

Good morning, Mom. Today I'm feeling a little doubt seeping in through my thoughts.

Doubt is a huge waste of energy. Please release it right now.

How?

The most simplistic way I can describe doubt, and why you need to let it go, is that it doesn't serve you. It wastes the importance of your now. Stop being so human. Be big, be wild, be bold. You need to believe. If you know in your heart that I can leave you dimes, why on Earth would you doubt that this book is meant to be?

Okay, I'm going to suspend this doubt.

Good. Let's move on. We have much more ambitious topics to acknowledge than doubt.

I'm very interested in expanding my knowledge while I'm here, so I don't waste a single moment talking about—as you said— things that don't serve me.

This is a great topic. Here's the thing. If you can direct your thoughts upon waking up toward the greater good, it will serve you all the days of your life, each and every day.

I really try to do this each morning.

Stop trying. Just do it. An easy exercise that will keep you on task is to write down empowering, positive, thankful thoughts before you go to bed. Keep it next to your bed. When you roll over in the morning, start with five minutes of quiet focused time on these thoughts. It will change the direction of the start of your new day. Many times, we hop up and the events of the day take over before the exchange of gratitude has a second to seep in—before coffee, before checking your phone, before talking out loud. Just be in a state of grace and gratitude, giving a nod to God.

I like this idea a lot. I have a gratitude project that I do each morning with my miracle partner, but I usually have to get my engine rolling before I do this.

It's important to not get your engine rolling. Allow yourself to be in an idle state of just being before anything else. This is your time with God. It may be the only real quiet moment you get with the Almighty all day. Be sure to welcome God to your day, your thoughts, actions, ideas, and daily life. Even when you are tying your shoes before your morning walk, you can speak with God and give thanks for the wonder of your nimble fingers.

Do we need to welcome God? Isn't God always there?

Yes, God is with you always. However, God is not here to force this loving energy in your direction. You must welcome it, which is no different than welcoming a house guest. If you want this love, ask for it.

CHAPTER FORTY

MASTER SOULS
AND FREE WILL

Good morning. I'm thinking about all of the master teachers that cross my path here and in The Next Room. How do these souls become so wise and elevated?

Exactly how you do. By listening, reading, praying, meditating, seeking, and tuning in God. They are no different than you or me. They just have spent more time, as you like to say, on peace rather than strife.

This brings me to a good point. I am amazed at the depth of childish behavior, hatred, and nasty divisiveness that seems prevalent in our society today, especially in politics.

It may be hard to believe, but all is well. This is the way the planet moves forward. What may seem nasty to you is just the way another expresses their care and concern. Do not waste your precious breath on trying to change anyone's opinion. Keep your thoughts focused on peace. You cannot change the direction to a positive flow with a negative thought.

This has been bothering me a lot lately.

It's just the ebb and flow of life. You will see clearly one day. So many aha moments await you.

Why do you think we can't get it together now?

Many do, and you have several moments where you have it "together." Free will is a complicated topic. You know in your heart that it's best to be loving, kind, and peaceful, but sometimes you just revert back to your old ways of lashing out and saying unkind things. Even if they remain unsaid—you may just think these thoughts—it's the same either way.

Do you mean saying something unkind and thinking something unkind have the same ability to damage someone?

Yes, although when it's spoken it is out in the open. A thought actually has the ability to cut deeper. That is why you must practice feeling good, no matter what. If you notice a negative thought, shake it out. Go outside, breathe deep, and count your blessings. You must do whatever you can to shake the bad thought away and focus on something new and happy.

Many might call this living in denial.

That is not the way we see it. It is transforming your soul to a state of bliss. Happiness, peace, kindness, and compassion are the way to be in communion with the Almighty. Ultimately, isn't that what you want?

Absolutely. I crave it.

Then stop worrying about anyone else's journey. This includes your husband and children. They have their own path to tread. Walk with God, Jane. This is the best place to hitch your wagon. By getting right with the Divine Loving Energy, you are right with everything.

I'm hoping I'm not being redundant with my thoughts. I'm just so happy that I have this open line of communication with you. Sometimes I wonder how on Earth I will get this all down and published.

You need only to trust. We see your heart. We know your passion to communicate with us. We know you are doing this to help others. Your intention from the beginning has been clear.

Why do you sometimes speak as Mom and then switch over and say "we?"

That is because I am bigger than just your mom. I have an entire host of heavenly spirits that are here with me, urging me to speak with you. We encourage you in getting this message out to your people. It's important that they hear this message, that they will never be punished, shamed, or blamed for their actions. They will be wrapped in love and given an opportunity to learn and expand in peace.

This makes me so happy. I'm not absolutely sure I'm capable of delivering all of this.

Oh, but you are. You are doing it right now. You are listening and translating. It is a shame you didn't learn to type faster.

Ha! I was such a bad typing student. I would hunt and peck as I watched my fingers, just like I'm doing now.

It's okay. You have actually gotten rather good at it. It's fun to watch you. Okay, onward.

Many times, I feel as though I may be misunderstood with all of this communicating with souls that have gone before me.

It matters not. Keep doing exactly what you're doing, sweetheart. It's an honor to be able to communicate through you.

You know, I just wrote the story about September 31, and on the calendar in front of me the date is September 30. So naturally I have been feeling you super close to me. It's been 10 years since you transitioned, and I miss you so much.

I'm right here. Just stop for a second. I will hug you.

I felt you! I could even feel your soft neck and smell your clean skin. I felt the veins on your hand as you reached for me. I heard your melodious voice in my ear speaking words of wisdom and comfort. It was a moment out of time. Thank you.

Anytime you need me, just call my name and I'll be there.

Another fabulous reference to a great song.

It's a pleasure for me to put things in a language that you are so familiar with and love. Music is so important to you. It always has been, even when you were a little girl. It soothed you.

I love hearing this, Mom. I don't think you've ever mentioned it before.

You would sit for hours at the piano listening to your sister, Gail, play. You loved the old hi-fi in the family room and always commented that you loved that we never turned it off, even when we left for a weekend. You always said that our home vibrated with the sounds of music. I'm sure your love affair with our friend, Torchie, was largely based on the fact that he played his stand-up bass many times in our home. You loved Torchie.

I really did. He was such a kind and lovely person. He was gentle too. He also saw me, even though I was a little girl. He looked at me and talked to me like a person, not just a little kid.

CHAPTER FORTY-ONE

September 31 Revisited

You transitioned exactly 10 years ago right now. I don't think I will ever recover from the pain of losing you.

Jane, I am not gone. I am simply out of sight for the time being. I am just in The Next Room. I'm not sure what it is about the human species, but you do seem to spend a lot of time grieving the loss instead of celebrating the life. Take the time necessary to perform your ceremonies and then wrap your arms around the living.

I know that, Mom, but it doesn't make days like this any easier.

Instead of remembering how I died and when, why not celebrate how I lived and all of the good times we had together?

I do, Mom. I guess I'm just thinking too much about the day you left. I remember calling the night before and you were feeling really weak and Dad was on the phone with me. I heard you in the background. I wish I could have told you one last time how much I love you.

You just did. You always told me you loved me but, even more than saying the words, the important part was in your actions. You always expressed yourself and showed me so much affection. You never pulled your hand away when I reached for it walking into the grocery store. You kissed my cheeks, rubbed my back, brushed my hair and never left my side when I needed you most. You were always available for me, as you are now. The pure fact that you are open enough to communicate with me right now is a gift.

Thank you for saying all of this. It actually gives me a lot of comfort.

Now that we have that out of the way, what is it you really want to talk about today?

Words and how important they are, and also how to choose them wisely. Today, as I was driving to the store, I saw a yard sign that said "No Hate Here," and although I understand what they were trying to say, I just feel it could be expressed more clearly.

Like perhaps, "Only Love Here"?

Yes, exactly.

Well, maybe the person with the "No Hate Here" sign is saying "Only Love Here" but that's how they choose to express their opinion. You possibly could still be smarting from the spanking you received using the word hate when you were just a child.

Yes, I believe you are right. I guess it's not that big of an issue. I just prefer the language of love.

You think too much. Get out of your own way and allow wisdom to flow directly from Source to your heart. If you would spend less time in your head thinking and the bulk of your time in your heart feeling, you would be able to achieve world peace. Alas, it's not to be during your lifetime, this time.

Will there ever be world peace?

Yes, but it may not be on this planet.

That just gave me a lot to mull over. I feel it's time to crack a bottle of bubbly, light a candle or two, and just sit with my favorite memories of you. I'll be back. I just need to honor you right now.

Take your time. I will be right next to you as you celebrate my life and our relationship. Many times, it's a good thing to step away and clear your head by aligning your heart.

CHAPTER FORTY-TWO

Music, Manifestation, and Memories

I loved going through my old photographs of us. I am really grateful that you made a point to visit me so often in California. There are so many great memories. I'm happy I have so much of it recorded in photos.

It was fun following you around. You have led a very exciting life, even though you have remained very down to earth and tied to your roots. I must admit I like your pace better now, though.

Yes, I've slowed way down. It suits me. I am early to bed and early to rise, which allows quiet time for prayer, gratitude, and spiritual alignment, all before a mindful walk/smell through the neighborhood with the pup. I feel my morning routine puts me into a perfect headspace to communicate with you. I am still surprised each time I sit down in my studio and open up this document. You are right here waiting for me.

Yes, I know. It's been my pleasure to show up for you. By the way, I'm loving your music selection today.

Jackie Gleason's Orchestra is one of my all-time faves. It's soothing and there's just something about his music that makes my heart soar.

You've always had a fondness for Big Band. It's a past-life situation for you.

Interesting. That has crossed my mind many times. It's like all of that music is embedded deep inside my cells. Okay, let's talk about manifestation.

Love it. Manifesting is one of the greatest and most fun gifts from the Divine.

Like the manifestation of our book. This project with you, even though it has changed forms and expanded over the past 10 years, is something that I dream about and think about daily.

This is exactly why you are sitting down to write every day (or at least most days). You are, in fact, manifesting this lifelong dream, and I am your guide to assist you in bringing your dream into the material world in real time.

I feel as though several times I have had individuals try to change the course or storyline of what I'm feeling.

Why on earth would you even talk about this project to anyone, other than those that you know have your back, believe in you, and will not alter or judge your passion?

I know, I need to get better about this. I just get so excited and filled with enthusiasm that sometimes I just overshare.

Show. Don't tell.

I really like that.

This story is unique because it is ours and ours alone. Try as you may, not everyone is going to understand that you are actually receiving messages from me, like the person you spoke to the other day. He really wanted you to bend this book into a physical version of The Next Room and you and I both know that it is an expression of the other side, not an actual room. If you change one word of our story you will be writing someone else's story, not ours. Understand?

Yes, yes, I do. I feel so much better now. I was truly considering changing our book to make it more of a novel and a fantasy, but what I know it to be is truth—my truth of connecting with you and to other souls that have gone before me.

I feel this is why you've been busying yourself with so many other things instead of being here in the studio writing, with your puppy at your feet. If it makes you feel better, you could always call the studio The Next Room. That adds a bit of solidness to The Next Room and it is, after all, where we are connecting.

Another great idea. Connecting with you in The Next Room in The Next Room!

As I mentioned to you previously, our book will not be for everyone and that is unquestionably okay. You are not writing this for "an audience." It is for you to break through and understand your life's passion and purpose. This book—our book—is for you and me, and for anyone else that cares to join us on this miraculous journey.

I'm brimming with gratitude right now. It always catches me by surprise when you are so straightforward and no B.S., just like when you were on this side.

That is because it is me. All me. Never, ever doubt that it is me.

I won't, Mom. Thank you.

CHAPTER FORTY-THREE

BAD DECISIONS AND A MAGIC WAND

It's a new day and deep sadness arrived as I think back on times in my life when I made terrible decisions and did not treat others or myself with respect and kindness.

I see your pain. You need to release these thoughts and stop beating yourself up. You have admitted these actions before God. That's all that needs to be done—awareness of your humanness and understanding that you are a good person in your heart. Perfection cannot be achieved while you are here. Please forgive yourself.

I'm not necessarily seeking perfection. I just want to work on being better on a daily basis.

We can see you are. You must know, Jane, that being the best you can be is a challenge minute by minute. The thoughts, actions, and decisions that are made are sometimes of an unconscious manner. It's interesting to me now as I can see the greater good and the bigger picture. What we need you to know is—all is well. It truly is. Stop right now and feel God's love. It will vibrate through each and every cell of your body. Forgiveness is For Giving to yourself. Give to yourself what you need to get this lesson because it is a big one. Give yourself grace, give yourself peace, give yourself love, give yourself understanding. Release the shame attached to the times that you refer to in your past. Please leave them there and embrace your now with a new perspective. It is this moment now that truly matters, right here, right now.

This helps immensely, and I'm feeling somewhat better. I was thinking about what each of you may be doing now that you're in The Next Room. As much as I like to think you and Dad are just hanging out, I have a feeling you're both on your own sojourn.

Yes, that's true. I was here waiting for your dad when he crossed. I helped him to know that everything I told him through Pam was true. I told him that I was just waiting in The Next Room while he finished his time on Earth. Once your dad found his footing, so to speak, I moved forward to my desired lessons and your dad moved along on his journey. We can and do cross paths whenever we choose, especially to celebrate with the family. Since our lives were joined together recently for 62 years, we are honored to look over the long, lasting legacy of love that we created while we were there with all of you.

Even though this past year was a crazy year, it was remarkable, too. We are so blessed with three new baby girls in the Asher extended family. All of this new life gives fresh energy and growth to our family. It's so lovely to see.

It is truly magnificent. Each one of those little baby girls is going to bring much renewed love and joy to the family. This, right here, is what truly matters and is important in the grand scheme of life. All of the other stuff should just fade away.

I wish that could be the case. I would love it so much if our family could all come together again, but I'm honestly not feeling that it's possible.

It is, although many of you may not witness it from your vantage point right now. You will see it from a greater perspective sooner or later. The younger members of the family understand that the strife and disagreements of the elders in the family was absolutely unnecessary. The issue is ego. They are too attached to what they think it should be, instead of loving what it genuinely is.

That's a good point. Sometimes I wish I had a magic wand, and I could make it all better.

It is not your job to make it all better. You are here to make your mark through your family, just like your dad and I did with all of you. As much as we wanted, your father and I could not bridge the disagreements within our own family. This is another reminder to "Let go, let God." I see that now more than ever. We are not here to fix anyone or anything. We are here to love. That is all.

It strikes me as such a simplistic answer, and I know it's true.

Love, love, and then love some more.

I'm ready to move on to another topic.

I'm ready. What is it that you would like to know?

Can we create or visualize our own passing?

That's a great question. The answer is yes, and no.

Yes and no?

Yes, because you can think about how you would like it to be and manifest your desires around your final exit. No, because you already decided how your passage out would be before you arrived.

That makes sense to me. I'm really hoping I chose to live a long healthy life so I can experience as much extended growth with my family as possible.

I hope so too.

Don't you know?

This is not a question for me.

You're right. Not fair.

It's not a matter of what's fair. It's not in my area of expertise. I am not your guide, your God, or your guardian. I am your mother. At least in this moment in time for this particular lifetime.

Okay, Mom. I get it. Thank you for setting me straight.

It is always my pleasure. I will always answer with my truth. It's all I have.

CHAPTER FORTY-FOUR

Grief and Good Energy

Hey! Thanks for the dime. It was such a clever spot to drop one. I had just been wondering why I hadn't seen one in a while, so it was super cool finding one next to my car seat. I love that each dime is always alone and in interesting spots.

You're welcome. It's always good to see you smile. Just like your smile right now.

It's my signature closed-lip smirk.

Yes, and I love it.

I am so happy that you're working on this project with me. I wonder sometimes what category it will be, other than non-fiction.

This matters not. Just keep writing and stay in your integrity. Leave this type of decision up to your publisher. That's what they know. When the time comes, it will be abundantly clear.

That's good advice. I had a bunch of thoughts on my walk this morning. My first thought is regarding the past year.

Yes, what would you like to know or discuss?

My recurring thought about 2020 is that it wasn't necessarily a "bad" year, even with all of the death and turmoil.

We agree. When you categorize an entire year by labeling it as bad or terrible, it takes away from all of the goodness and mercy that is nestled in each and every moment. This is what we'll say about 2020. It was unquestionably necessary for each of you living through this time. It is going to wake many of you up. It is going to be a time of creative growth and great love. It is going to be a time of discovery and deep intuitive gifts. It is your time to shine and use your knowledge about what you're learning for the betterment of humankind. This is what you signed up for, this shift in consciousness. It is the great awakening. Although it has been jarring, abrupt, and full of change with extensive grief, it still holds tender beauty and gentle grace.

I really feel this, and every time I see something negative about 2020, including COVID, politics, lack of income or death, I work at finding the light in the situation instead.

That is inspired and exactly what all of your guides, guardian angels, and mother want you to see. I do not mean to make light of the situation, but if you don't have anything nice to say, don't say it.

Exactly. This is circling back to our earlier discussion about staying in our own lane, yes?

Yes. You can never focus enough good energy and love in this direction. You must keep loving the unlovable. Continue to pray for those that profess that they do not want protection. You must continue to send light and love everywhere, all day, every day. It's a rare opportunity on the planet to embrace this generosity of spirit and to shine your light bright for others to see. We are counting on all of you to break through to the other side with an expanded consciousness in a delightful way.

Let's talk about happiness.

Happiness is a great space to reside, although the feeling of being contented is like slipping on a comfortable old shoe.

Whenever you are out of alignment with feeling good, literally stop what you are doing, sit quietly, and think about all of the things that restore your level of fulfillment.

I totally get that, but sometimes I feel so down and blue. The best way to describe this feeling is that, when you left, you took all of the bright colors with you and left my world a little grey.

I am not going to tell you to move on or get over it. What I will say about grief is that it is something that you must learn to live with. The depth of your grief is directly tied to the amount of love you've witnessed and experienced. This is not just tied to me but through your dad, Lynn, Budgie, your cousins, aunts and uncles, and others who have transitioned. You have been a very fortunate soul in this lifetime, and you are deeply loved and admired. This is why your pain feels so grey, and, years after I've gone from your sight, you still think of me and feel empty, lost and deeply sad. I know it's not all the time but know I had these feelings about my mother, too. It's just that life is for the living. You must not spend your days dwelling on those of us that have moved on.

It's just that I feel so tied to you. It feels different with you not here with me, even though I know I will see you again.

You will. There is much life to live and lead between now and then. Get busy living, Jane.

I am. I love my husband, children, puppy, family, and friends very much. I do feel remarkably blessed. I know what I need to work on. I'm so very aware of the gifts I've been given, and of being able to speak with you through my heart and write down your words.

It is a gift—one that you are receiving because you asked for it and you believe it to be true. I'm going to repeat this for you again. I may have transformed and left from your sight over 10 years ago, but I never, ever left your side, not once.

I am with you as I am with all of my children, grandchildren, and great grandchildren. Many people in the family speak to me, and some do not. It's a choice. It doesn't make me any closer to anyone in particular. It just brings them closer to me. Do you understand?

I think what you're saying is that you are equally available for each of us, even if some of us bring you closer through our thoughts, words, and actions to ourselves. Is that right?

Yes, exactly! You are no more special than anyone else in this family. It's just that you choose to communicate with me openly and you're unafraid of what anyone thinks of you regarding our communication.

Gee, make a girl feel special.

I know you're teasing. You also know what we mean to one another and so do I. This isn't a contest, Jane. Love cannot be measured. In its purest form it is God. Each and every one of us has the ability to have more love, which, in essence, is more God. You are actively seeking this communication with me, that's all. Many others are seeking it too. You're just open and outspoken about it.

That makes sense. I often want to talk to other family members about writing this book with you, but I stop short. I need to continue on my path and show instead of tell, as you said earlier.

Yes, please do. This is really not something that you are able to educate someone about. This is your truth, your intuition, your conscious and unconscious connection to the Divine. Please revel in it. Speak your truth, but please don't try to bend anyone toward what you are feeling. It is important to allow each person in your life to feel their own feelings and find their own truth. This is why many times you attract complete strangers, which are not actually strangers but friends from another time that you recognize. You are able to speak more freely with these individuals that you bond with because they are in your tribe but not your family. Does this make sense to you?

Yes, very much so. I relate to individuals that I have never laid eyes on in person. I have many close relationships with these twin souls. It allows me to understand how deeply we are all connected.

Yes. We are all one. God designed it beautifully. This mastery of love is the vibrational pull that links each and every soul to one another. When a brother or sister hurt, you feel it on a deep and spiritual level. Even if you don't think you are affected, you are, although you may not realize it in the moment. This is not a judgment, it's just part of your evolutionary process as a soul during this lifetime.

What about empaths?

It is a very interesting time for these old souls that are intuitive, tuned in, and aware of the energy of the planet and the multitude of issues at the moment. The wisest of them will stay in peace. They will not engage or argue, no matter what the topic may be. They are the individuals that stand their ground in peace even when someone may accuse them of not standing up for something through their silence. They are standing up— they are standing up for peace. Do you see?

Yes, I do. This moment in time has been very polarizing. I choose not to play.

Good. It's healthier this way. It may seem as though you're looking through rose-colored glasses but truly, what's wrong with that? Please continue to search for the unicorn, keep looking up for a sky full of rainbows, and keep sending those love letters to the universe. It is honestly the healthiest way to enjoy this big, bountiful life that you've been blessed to live this time around.

It's like that quote from Paul Coelho: "The world is changed by your example, not by your opinion."

Yes, another remarkable example of show, don't tell.

CHAPTER FORTY-FIVE

Healing the Planet and Boundaries

Happy Monday! Today I woke up feeling really refreshed and blessed.

Doesn't it feel wonderful when that happens?

Yes, it does. While I was on my walk, I was thinking about how exciting it is that I'm writing this book with you, and I'm feeling really tuned in to what you're allowing me to see, feel, and hear.

I'm glad to hear this. Continue to pray and give thanks. This will keep your heart wide open to all of the grace and expansive goodness that is always available and flowing to you. The more open you are, the more available you are to receive the signs and messages. They feel welcome to land softly in your heart without hesitation.

It sounds rather simple.

That's because it is. It's profoundly simple and uncomplicated. Human beings like to make things a big deal when they truly are not. Yes, there are things that you view as big issues on the planet, but how you approach them and the energy you give them is where the importance lies. It is time to listen. The planet is speaking to us. It is enjoying this break and regenerating right now. It is using God's gifts of the sun and wind, and moving humanity forward with wise ecological uses of its natural energy.

I love that the planet is able to heal and rejuvenate. I'm also in awe of God's magnificence in showing us how to use natural resources for energy.

Yes. God the Almighty Energy of All is smiling right now.

I'm going to switch topics on you again. What if you have had an issue with someone and neither of you have faced each other or offered an apology?

You can clear the air from a distance. It's not actually necessary to always do this face to face. Give this individual the space they need by sending them love and light. They will feel this good energy flow to them, and the issue will resolve itself on its own. Occasionally, the pain of a disagreement can cut deep, and it's hard for you to reconnect and be as close as you once may have been, and that's okay. It's important to not harbor ill will or negative feelings toward this individual. Resentment will only result in you stunting your own growth as an evolving human being. You must allow love to flow, no matter what transpired. Love is the only thing that matters. Being right does not matter, and blame does not belong in any situation. By allowing yourself to grow, you can't help but to move yourself forward in a positive manner. All of these so-called disagreements, troubles, trials, and arguments are all placed in our path so we can continue to grow into wiser, more loving beings.

I love that answer so much, Mom. I'm really working on this one. It's hard because of the emptiness I feel from the loss of friendship, but I know it's best to love from a distance.

Boundaries are important as long as they are not created to cut off the flow of love. Whenever you withhold love for another you are essentially cutting off the flow of love to yourself.

I understand. I will continue to work on this one.

Good! What's next?

I've been thinking about how we accumulate so much stuff throughout our lives, and how we always seem to want more, just to donate, sell, or give it away at a later date.

Isn't that the truth. None of that "stuff" is important—not your home, car, possessions, money in the bank. It's all just a bunch of illusions that perhaps enhance your life experience, but in the grand scheme of things are not at all relevant.

From your elevated perspective, what do you consider important?

The relationships you develop with others, including the love of family and friends, kindness for everyone you encounter, helping others with your generosity and gifts. And the most important thing of all is your relationship with God. All the rest of the stuff are just insignificant trappings.

I get this but it is also so fun to update our homes and drive a nice car. I know it sounds weird, but I really love my car. I have wanted a convertible since I owned my little M.G. in 1983. Every time I walk out in the garage and look at Flo— I say, "Hello, Flo" and smile. Does this make me shallow?

No, just human. We are wired to like nice things and to pursue them whether it is a new chair, a comforter, front door, new carpet, a beautiful sweater, or a new vehicle. There is nothing wrong with liking new things. It's when you allow the quest of "things" to take over that it becomes an issue. We must always view these items as just the extra cushion on a life well lived. I believe Oprah mentioned that the first time she realized she could buy whatever she wanted. What she longed for was quality towels and nice bedding. The old phrase, "home is where the heart is," could possibly be why we love to fuss over our space. It's where we live, love, laugh, cry, play, and share our deepest desires. Of course, we want our space to represent who we are. It's the outer shell of our softer inside. By the way, Flo feels your love. She feels you smile each time you get behind the wheel. You didn't purchase her as a status symbol. You genuinely wanted to be happy when you drive. This, my dear, is called the pursuit of happiness.

I really am happy when I drive her. I drive so very little these days, I figured, why not smile while I'm doing it? Okay, so we can't take it with us, right? What about giving things away?

I'm a fan, as you well know. You were on the receiving end of many of my things while I was still on the other side. I consider giving with a warm hand to be quite admirable. You get to physically see someone enjoy the gift that you've handed to them. It's especially meaningful when you know that the receiver actually loves the item you are giving them. For instance, my mother's locket. When you were a little girl, you would look at that locket for hours and hold it in your little hand. When I asked you what you wanted for your 21st birthday, you told me a locket. You were not asking for your grandmother's locket, rather a new locket. I decided then and there that you needed to have my mother's locket. When I told your dad, he cleaned it up and we bought a new chain and then added the picture of your grandmother inside. This was a gift from the heart, one I know that you have now given to your daughter, Betty. To consider that possibly many moons from now your great granddaughter may wear this inexpensive but meaningful locket from the late 1800s is rather fascinating.

CHAPTER FORTY-SIX

GOSSIP AND GOOD PEOPLE

On my walk this morning, the topic of gossip popped in my head.

It is the most unnecessary form of communication there is. Simply stop doing it. Even when you think you are sharing innocent information about one friend to another, if it isn't unmistakably seeped in love then those words should remain bottled up and never spoken. Do you understand?

Yes, I do. It's not always easy, especially when I know people that I find highly entertaining that say things like, "If you don't have anything nice to say, come sit by me."

I'm going to have to be unrelenting about this one. These are not your people. Gently let them go. Release them back into the wild to find their own gossip tribe. You, my daughter, do not need this type of influence in your life—ever.

I know, Mom. It's easier now that I work from home. As much as I loved the radio business, there were many times I would cringe when the negative conversations started. Conversely, I have many uplifting, fun, and highly entertaining radio friends that don't gossip. The radio business is based on communication, and sometimes it was not always the highest form of communication.

Good people are everywhere, Jane. Surround yourself with the best people. This will allow you to bring forth your highest good. This is not to say that you are better than anyone else. It's about choice. If you want to elevate and grow, you must have conversations with people about the very things you desire.

I really get this. I've been very fortunate because in writing our book and recording my shows for The Next Room podcast, I have instinctively surrounded myself with those that want to dig deep into the meaning of life and what comes next. I've always been fascinated by these topics and so to meet other inspired individuals is a great blessing.

Your podcast is helping people. Continue to do your show. It's meaningful.

I will, and I do know it's helping people. I was thinking about my little friend, Budgie, on my walk. I'm wondering why she left so quickly and at such a young age. Can you help shed light on this?

I can, but to be honest, you already know. She did not leave as quickly as you may perceive. She knew, due to complications with her illness, that she was not going to live a long, extended life. She's okay with this. She changed so many lives for the better in the short time she was in human form. She had completed her work this time around. She's an extraordinary soul, which I have so enjoyed knowing and continue to connect with now. She's a friend that you'll be forever linked to through lifetimes of understanding and growth.

Thank you for saying that about Budgie. I often find myself thinking of her and it surprises me when I remember that she is no longer here on this side.

Just like me, she is with you always. Call upon her, tune in and listen. Although she has many other people that she needs to watch over and connect with, she is available for you as well.

Like the time my iTunes started playing *Take It Easy* the second I asked her a question?

Yes, exactly like that. She knew how important it was for you to say goodbye and pray with her one last time, so that is why she waited for you.

I know, Mom. It was the most incredible thing that has ever happened to me regarding someone's death. She gave me an enormous gift allowing me to hold her hand and pray the Lord's Prayer with her as she took her final breath. As difficult and as painful as that was to witness, I remember it in great loving detail as a divine reward from my little Budgie.

I'm happy you had the opportunity to be with her. I know how you longed to stay by my side, but I knew you had to go home to your family. You had been by my side every day for weeks as I chose to recover. As I have told you time and time again, life is for the living.

Getting on the plane was the hardest thing I have ever done, even though you had officially been moved to rehab. I look back and wish with all my might that I could have stayed longer.

Why? There is nothing you or anyone could have done for me.

I guess just to have more time holding your hand. That would have been really nice.

Think of all the times we did hold hands. Literally thousands of times. Hold these memories in your heart and know that I am with you now. Let's move on. I like to see you smile, remember?

It's All Souls' Day, and on my walk this morning I named everyone that I could think of who has gone before me. It makes me realize how much love I have been given and how many wonderful people have crossed my path.

Isn't it wonderful to think about all these individuals and to bring their faces into your mind's eye? When you experience the love of those here and now and those in The Next Room, it is quite astonishing to receive this dual level of vibrational love. When you are wrapped in the love of both sides, it will help you to understand the depth of our never-ending lifetime-after-lifetime bond.

CHAPTER FORTY-SEVEN

Alignment and Puzzle Pieces

Today I want to talk about this book and how to get this story aligned.

You are thinking too much about it. You honestly need to just allow this to happen. Everything about this book is as natural as your birth. You need to just be. It is in you. I am in you. This conversation we are having is all part of the grand design of you doing what you were put on earth to do. You are so fortunate to be standing up and answering the call.

What do you mean by that?

What I mean is, you are doing it. You are writing our story. You are associating with me on a deeper, more spiritual level and allowing this book to channel through you. You cannot possibly get it wrong because it is what you know and believe. Don't you see?

I do. Especially at moments like now when I feel you so near to me and I hear your voice in my ear. It's like you are sitting right beside me.

It is because I am. Do you remember your friend, Sarah, telling you last week that you were showing up and doing this and how happy she was for you? This is the type of encouragement you need from someone you respect as both a professional and a friend. You are very lucky that you have gathered a great group of individuals that believe in you. This will bolster your confidence to continue to allow this book to progress from you into the light of day.

I'm not sure how to begin our story, though. I have so many unfinished chapters and I seem to get stuck on everything leading up to the communication that we are having right now.

You positively do know how to begin our story. Just tune in and it will come to you, just like what we are doing in this very moment. Please go back to trust and I will help you.

I have tears in my eyes right now. Of course, you have been here with me every step of the way, so why wouldn't you help with the beginning of our book? I feel so relieved. Just like the relief Dad felt when he realized why he was feeling so strange after you died. That conversation was intrinsically sad but deeply profound. His realization rendered me speechless and I felt our collective misery merge together over losing you. What's amazing is that he knew you better than anyone.

Yes, he did. He is my best friend. We really had a wonderful life together and we still do. Even when we were on your side, we had a few bumps along the way but we continued to hold hands and together created a magnificent family filled full of good people with kind hearts.

I feel really honored to have been a witness to your love. It has taught me about strength and to believe in my own relationship with Tom, no matter what challenges we face along the way. Being part of a loving relationship is extremely empowering.

It is, for you. However, not everyone needs to be in a relationship of marriage. We were designed as human beings to have a pack—to be with others, to surround ourselves with love. Not everyone wants a one-on-one love, and this is why they do not manifest this type of relationship.

That makes sense.

Free will, remember? If they truly wanted to be in a one-on-one, they would create one. Sometimes people prefer to be alone and so they build a different sort of family, one of friendships. Don't ever feel sorry for someone because they have a different type of love in their life. It's all love. It really depends on the needs of each individual. Looking over my life as your mom, I can see it was important for me to have a very large family with many connections. It was my choice this time around.

I have many friends that say they would like to be in a loving relationship.

Just remind them that they can be. If they truly desire this, it will come. They, just like you, create their current reality.

I will. Okay, Mom, would you like to go back to the beginning of our story and start organizing what I have written so far and assist me in pulling all of the puzzle pieces together?

Yes, let's do it.

CHAPTER FORTY-EIGHT

Back to the Beginning and Afterlife

Thank you so much! I really felt you were beside me as I worked on Part One of our book and got it organized. I feel so much better about everything.

You're welcome, sweetheart. It's important to get our story down from the beginning as it leans into our communication that we are enjoying in our now. So, what are we to discuss today?

My grief.

I felt your sadness on your walk this morning, as I can feel it now. I wish I could help you to really see what I see, so that you would realize this deep sadness that you carry in your heart does not have to feel so heavy.

I wish you could show me, too. I'm really trying, but today for some reason I felt so sad at not physically being able to see you and talk to you and hold your hand or have an afternoon cocktail with you. I just feel so darn empty and I couldn't stop these feelings from taking over my heart. Why today? Why now? It's been over 10 years and you would think that I would be able to control these emotions better by now.

First of all, why are you trying to control anything? You need to allow your life to flow and you need to just be my darling girl. There is nothing wrong with getting emotional or welling up when you think of me. Once again, I will tell you this is because of the undeniable closeness we shared when I was still with you on the other side. We remain close now. Don't let this slow you down. Embrace this new way of our connection and communication and continue to let it grow deeper and more meaningful each day.

I am trying. It just amazes me when it sneaks up on me, like this morning.

This is just your perception of sadness. Feel what you must feel and then give it the space to move on. This so-called sadness is renting space. You can change your thoughts at any moment and release it.

This is such a great reminder of being able to pivot our thoughts. The biggest theme that seems to be playing on a loop is the recent election and all of the divisiveness and arguments taking place across social media and in public.

Don't do it.

Don't do what?

Engage in the disagreements or arguments. When you stand in peace, you are standing for the most important stance instead of arguing your truth, as there is no point whatsoever trying to change someone's perception or opinion. It doesn't work that way. You must stay in balance, stay in love, stay in peace. You are not here to decide how someone else should think or feel, so do not react to their story. Stay in a space of knowing all is well, no matter how much you feel you need to engage and try to prove your point of view.

I often think about how you raised us. You gave us a solid foundation, but I do not ever recall you telling me that others were wrong if they disagreed with your philosophy.

Your dad and I raised all of you in a conservative home with traditional values. Although we held our political views privately, we also honored our friends and neighbors who had a differing point of view. We never forced our beliefs, political or religious, on anyone. We did not feel that was our place. We raised the six of you in our beliefs until you were all old enough to be on your own and gather your own thoughts of the world.

I am forever grateful that after I explored the left coast and came home with a wide berth of new ideas and thoughts, you and Dad never tried to change me or make me fit back into the mold of how you raised me. I felt respected and honored and heard when I brought up a topic that I was curious about.

(Laughs) Yes, your dad and I worried for about a half a heartbeat but then realized that you were here helping to elevate our perspective of the world, too. As you grew, we grew.

My foundation was strong, thanks to the two of you.

You also have great faith and amazing friends. Your connection to our family is unshakable. We knew we needed to let you go to let you grow.

I'm just amazed at how much anger people have on both sides of the political aisle. This is what I don't understand. How did we get here as a society?

All of what is happening right now is just growing pains. Please do not view this as bad or good. It just is. It is important to empathize with an opposite view than your own. All of this is about our growth as a civilization on this planet. Be wide open, curious and not judgmental. Being able to understand why someone is so upset over an election not going their way is part of a process, just as it is every single time there is an election. Many people did not understand or agree with the changes that were made four years ago, but it was also necessary for our growth. Each time we move forward, even if it appears that it is a step backward, know that it is not. It's not possible to go backward. A different perspective and understanding has already been revealed.

Oh, I like that explanation a lot.

Good. It helps to have an elevated overview from The Next Room. Not that I am above you in any sense of the word. I just have a unique and broadened vantage point to learn from now.

I appreciate these lessons very much. Do you see or feel that we have to live in fear right now because of all of the dissension?

No, not in the least. There is still much more love, kindness, compassion, and goodness that far outweigh the negative reactions that you may be hearing, reading, or experiencing right now. Please do not buy into the illusion. This is exactly what the individuals that enjoy being angry are banking on. Do not be led by fear.

Again, good advice. I honestly feel the invisible hand of the Holy Spirit over my mouth when I want to respond to some of the silliness I hear and read on social media.

You are much better served to look for another opportunity to uplift someone. Is there a way for you to do a good deed—something only between you and the individual in need? Write a letter. Call a friend. Take a walk. Pray. Breathe deep. Pray some more. Prayer is the most powerful action that you can possibly take. Here lies the beauty of a ritual steeped in grace. To pray without ceasing is a love song to the Almighty.

These nuggets of wisdom are inspiring me daily.

I'm happy to help. What would you like to speak about now?

The Afterlife.

Well, now, that is certainly right up my alley. What about it?

Well, every single person I speak to has a different view of what comes next.

Yes, of course they do. That's what makes life so interesting. This one and the next one and so on. To listen and allow others to express their ideas, opinions, knowledge, instinct, or religious beliefs is a gift. This is not something that needs commenting on, just pure acceptance. Everyone needs to get to their place of understanding, whether it happens on that side or in The Next Room.

I always find it fascinating when I ask the question for my podcast, "What do you feel is in The Next Room?" The answers are as varied as they are fascinating.

Of course. If you would have asked me this question before I transitioned it would have been completely different than my understanding of what my truth is now.

Did this surprise you?

I don't think surprise is quite the term I would use. I think it was more of a fulfilled, built-in aha moment. It didn't feel odd; more of an awakening to what I knew all along but perhaps forgot in my earthly form. The one thing I will add is that having faith really helped me see things quickly after I left. I already believed in the Afterlife even though I wasn't exactly sure what it would look or feel like. I had the Bible as my point of reference. What I will say is that it is even more beautiful, expansive, and inspired than I could have ever dreamed of in my wildest notions.

CHAPTER FORTY-NINE

It's Not Work
if You Love It

Hey, Mom. It's been a while. Getting ready for Thanksgiving gives me a whole new appreciation for everything you did for our big family of eight year after year. It's remarkable how you cooked, cleaned, laughed, and prepared everything as though it were magic. My family is half the size, and it is so much work.

It's not work if you love it, and there is nothing magical about the dedication to family and rolling up your sleeves to get cracking. I enjoyed it very much. There's nothing like looking around the table at the love of your life (or many lifetimes) and the beautiful people that you've created together. It still makes me smile thinking about the nightly dinners gathered around the table in Deckerville. Hands folded, heads bowed, reciting, "Come, Lord Jesus . . ." before a bite was taken. Giving thanks is such an important thing to do daily, minute by minute. I had so very much to be grateful for and I still do, even more so now as I watch our beautiful family grow.

It's really such a huge blessing. To think you have a great, great granddaughter through Elizabeth, and two more great granddaughters! Marcie's little girl was just born, and

Kristen's is on the way after Christmas—2020 has been the year of the woman for the Asher tribe.

Yes, it has. So much wisdom to be learned from these little ones. Please be sure to listen.

I will, although the long distance and this virus is going to keep me from meeting them for a while.

Don't worry about that. You'll recognize one another when you do finally meet. What shall we discuss today?

Truth.

Great topic. Go ahead. What is it you would like to know?

Well, on my walk this morning, I thought about writing a prologue to our book to talk about my truth about what this is that we are doing.

Do it. I have only one thought. Please don't apologize for what your truth is. It is yours. What you are hearing, feeling, and knowing intuitively is categorically your truth. Our book absolutely needs a prologue and an epilogue. This is not the only one, you know. We will collaborate on at least one or two more books together, depending on how busy you will be. I can't do this alone. I need you, Jane.

I need you too, Mom. More than words can say. As of this writing, it is December 10, 2020 and, as I prepare for a very different-looking Christmas, I am missing you even more. You really had a way of making the holidays special. I wrote a piece about you for Facebook, and many people responded and loved it.

I know. I was with you as you were writing it. Thank you for all of your kind words and keen observations. I will say that being a Christmas fairy came naturally to me, as I love to see my loved ones smile. You happen to be a very good Christmas fairy yourself.

That's because I had an amazing teacher. I'm going to put this aside for the moment and go write about my truth.

It's important so I can dig into our book. I'm feeling very motivated to get this finished and published.

It's never going to be finished in the way you think. This is an on-going story that will be told for generations, as long as someone is willing to connect and write everything down.

I love that thought. Thank you.

CHAPTER FIFTY

MOTHER TIME
AND MOTHER-IN-LAW

Here we are—the 16th of December 2020. Time has a way of getting away from me.

It gets away from everyone, Jane. Time waits for no one. That's why it is such a precious gift to give someone your time, make a call, send a note, drop in for a visit. Giving someone your time is truly the most selfless act we have. Just like you are giving me your time, right now.

Another great song reference, this time the Rolling Stones. You make me smile, Mom. I would love to have had you with us as while shopping with my mother-in-law, Frances, in Palm Desert yesterday.

Oh, but I was there. I was in the car with you when you told her that I was with you. You even glanced at the empty seat in the back next to you as you envisioned me right there in the car. Even though this concept may be difficult for others to completely grasp, I know you knew I was right there. I loved that you told her the feather story and how she seemed surprised we would have a cocktail at lunch time. It was cute. I love that woman. You are extraordinarily blessed that you have her in such good health right now. Please listen to her—she's very wise. She also understands all of this, even though she does have moments when a little doubt sneaks into her thoughts. This doubt is not of her faith but of how easy it is for you and me to communicate with one another. She's curious and cautiously optimistic. She's going to have so much fun when she gets here. Time is not a perfect science or easy to gauge, but it feels like she is a long way off from joining me.

I'm happy to hear you say that. I feel as though she's going to be around a long time, too. I at least hope and pray this to be true, although no one ever knows. She's been such a wonderful support for me. I treasure our conversations. She's a big supporter of my podcast and she's really shown interest in our book. I am honored by her fascination and belief in me. Not everyone shows interest.

It's a difficult topic for people to grasp. Stop waiting for anyone to take interest and just keep writing. That is your ego talking. Please let it go.

Thank you for that advice.

What's on your mind today?

Well, I've been thinking about the vastness of The Next Room. Try as I might, it's a never-ending quest to try and understand exactly what it will be like.

You need to allow it to be what it is, without trying to define what it is. There is no way that you can possibly grasp the depth and properly capture in your words what this experience is like. It's beyond any thoughts that you've had. Many times, you've had magnificent dreams where you fly, time-travel, or visit with those of us that have moved beyond. Even your dreams where you leap from treetops and watched dimes spin into hundred-dollar bills, all while you travel in spaceships and land them with ease. These fantastical dreams are magical and amazing but are barely scratching the surface of the experience of The Next Room.

I have to stop trying to figure it out because I do understand that there really is no way of knowing it until I join you, which is hopefully a long time from now!

We have covered so many important topics and I want to see you complete our book. This will open the door and then you will grow in confidence and faith to take our Next Room Two to the next level.

That's exciting, Mom. All I want to do is write. It soothes my soul.

It's what I feel you were meant to do.

Do you have any final thoughts?

Keep loving what is right in front of you. Stop searching. The need to seek any answers can be found in your heart. Be still and know that you have everything you could possibly want or need. Love is the answer to everything. When in doubt, love the person, place, or situation even more, even when what is presented before you doesn't appear lovable. Believe me, it is. There is always room for more love. Breathe it in, exhale it out. Love here and now, forever and always.

Working with you heart to heart on our book has brought us even closer than I ever imagined possible. I honestly don't want it to end.

It will never be the end, Jane. Our relationship will continue, on and on. Please keep talking to me and continue to get quiet and tune in. We both know there is much more to our story from The Next Room.

I love you, Mom.

I love you too, sweetheart.

Epilogue

As my mother previously expressed, this book is not the end, for there is no end. This is a story of lifetimes woven from delicate threads of consciousness over multitudes of generations who traveled before me. In this moment right now, we are one, as well as many future moons from now. We'll continue to evolve together as one.

I reflect over a session I had several years ago with Pam when I first started receiving answers through her. In this particular session, Mom showed Pam a multitude of various beings, not necessarily all human. I remember the feeling that took over my senses that day, not exactly fear but rather of disbelief and unease. In that moment, I was not ready to grasp the vast idea of these "other-worldly" entities sharing The Next Room with her, even though intellectually I knew this to be true. It's still so much easier to imagine The Next Room as Heaven—like with all of our loved ones laughing, learning, and playing on an elevated level. In this magical place, dogs are frolicking and flowers are blooming everywhere with background music playing that is felt rather than heard.

Mom sensed my trepidation and she quickly switched gears and eased me back gently into the still water of what she knew I could grasp, which is what you've just read. During that session with Pam, she referred to Light Beings and Soul Energies from other lifetimes. What exactly does that mean? I feel as though I'm about to find out. It's now the intrinsic matter of me truly getting out of my own way. I know now that it is time for me to expand beyond my humanness and trust Mom to gently guide me through our next fascinating waltz through The Next Room—Two.

Acknowledgments

As my mother has pointed out time and again. We are forever connected by an invisible thread of love, here, and beyond in *The Next Room*. This book was possible because of each and every one of these threads. My deepest gratitude begins with…

- You, mom, I am thankful for your direct style of communication and for showing up so we could write this book together. Our deep loving relationship continues to inspire me across our *many* lifetimes together.
- Dad, for your open mind and insistence in speaking with Pam shortly after mom left our side. Without your generosity this book may have taken me even longer to publish. Thanks for sending the butterflies too.
- Lynn Marie, for your pragmatism, friendship, and the initial spark of inspiration to ask Pam if she would be involved. You are the world's greatest big sister.
- My little Budgie, thank you for providing me the name of my podcast and book but especially for waiting for me to hold your hand before you exited for The Next Room. Every time I see a heart, I think of you. ♥
- My husband for your unfettered belief in me. There's no way this project would ever see the light of day without your unyielding love, support and daily deliveries to the studio of dark chocolate. I'll always remember

what you said to me just as the pandemic hit when I had lost a big client. I asked you about what I should do next, and you said; "Jane, it's a perfect time for you to write your flipping book." Thank you, my love, you are *my one and only*.

- To the magical Pam Oslie, your willingness and generosity with dad to translate messages from Mom and for your open heart and passionate desire to help people heal on their life's sojourn here *and beyond*. You always said yes to me, no matter the question, or favor. This book would not be the same without you.
- Yoda, thank you for your intuitive inspiration 11 years ago.
- My niece Marcie, for your consistency with encouragement and love.
- Sarah Seidelmann, my mystical motivational shaman, you listened and believed as you held a safe space for me to share my story beginning to end.
- My extraordinary children, who fill my heart with a daily dose of unconditional love and understand that it's a good thing to talk to our loved ones who have only changed forms. And for the many hugs and belly laughs. I am so happy we are connected now and forever.
- To my editing hawk-eye Kevin Bradley, for your keen observations and desire to be a willing participant on this journey. For your gentle suggestions and expertise which made you an invaluable part of our team. Mom says thank you too.
- Sweet Jo, (*My miracle partner*) for opening your heart, ears and arms to embrace me day in and day out as I explored the limitless possibilities of turning this idea into solid form. Your assistance in the first rounds of grammar and punctuation was so appreciated!

- To the fabulous Carla from Clarity Designs for your efficiency, professionalism and effortless organizational skills. You took our edited manuscript from an authentic story and wove it into a gorgeous book. To borrow a phrase from another one of your clients…You indeed breathe awesomeness!

- To Burrows and Sweet Rose, your drawings and support for this book added energy, whimsy and depth to *The Next Room*. It's good to have the Burrows Creative team to call on.

- My beautiful Mother-in-law, Frances you supported me and have been fully invested in my podcast from day one. I love you, Snookie.

- My fab girlfriend Nancy Newcomer for your listening ear and eagerness to look over the final draft. You are the typo queen and have been a trusted confidant along my path of self-discovery.

- To my Bestie, Nancy Schoenheide, for listening over the years and assisting me by allowing me to find my own way. Thank you for believing in me, and for *not* helping me…even when I asked. ☺

- Teri Citterman, I recall the first time I told you I was writing a book, you asked me what it was about, and then…you listened, thank you.

- Terry (Jimmy) Jaymes, thank you for opening my mind to unique possibilities of connection when we met and now, for reading the advance of *The Next Room*, *as well as* the offer to interview me on all of your various media outlets. Your friendship inspires me.

- To my new friend Casey Gauntt…make no mistake, Jimmy orchestrated our introduction through the fabulous Jesse B., Jesse, *thank you.* Casey, we've only just begun.

- To Brent Carey, for your belief and encouragement to create a podcast about my passion, you and Empower Radio are a massive gift. I am honored to be part of your family and your dream, deep gratitude for my ace producer, Tony Facchini too!
- Jan Warner, from the second you agreed to come on my podcast our friendship grew. Your ability to open your heart and hold space for millions of fans and followers through "Grief Speaks Out," thank you for keeping it real, compassionate and kind.
- To my supportive and loving siblings: Gail, Patti, Donna and Tom. I love each of you, dearly. I appreciate your interest and timely questions surrounding this labor of love.
- And for all of my friends and family who tuned in and listened along the way, my cousin Anne, thank you for your belief in me, Big Al for telling me…ever so gently as we walked along the Pacific to get out of my own way, Janie D. for rooting for me and listening, always listening, Catalina, my little sister of laughter and light, you get me, to Santa Barbara for cheering me on throughout the years and sending content and ideas my way for the podcast, you rock… and to my Sister-in-Law Mimi, your excitement for this book is infectious.
- And last but certainly not least, to all of my Facebook Fans, Twitter followers, podcast listeners and believers everywhere, I am bathed in a warm glow of gratitude for your kindnesses. Ludovico Einaudi, your music transcends me to another level and you have been my daily background as I wrote, wept and brought our story to life. And finally to Mamba, my muse and puppy at my feet, mommy loves you.

About the Author

Jane Asher has always been a natural connector who has enjoyed a successful career in media and the music industry, most notably at major radio stations in San Diego and Santa Barbara, and Virgin Records based out of Chicago.

Several years ago, she stepped away from terrestrial radio when Empower Radio reached out and asked her to create a show regarding her passion. *The Next Room* podcast was born. She interviews professionals and practitioners from diverse backgrounds about death, dying, grief, beliefs and cultural traditions surrounding the journey we all must ultimately make. The show airs across 11 platforms and has connected her with extraordinary people throughout this community. *The Next Room* has recently been named the official podcast of the Beautiful Dying Expo.

Jane is also drawn to mission work. She has been part of a team for five years that has built homes in Tijuana for families in need through Lutheran Border Concerns. She has traveled to El Salvador to feed the homeless, Malaysia to help build a school on Borneo, and Armenia to work with women and children in the village of Amre Taza. Most recently, she was on a humanitarian mission in the Dominican Republic.

Jane lives in San Diego with her husband, Tom. She is now answering her passion-filled purpose and writing daily alongside her puppy and muse, Mamba.

To find out more about Jane, visit janeasherreaney.com

UNTIL WE MEET AGAIN...
IN THE NEXT ROOM

Mom, Dad, Lynn and Honey,
Grandma & Grandpa Harmon, Grandma & Grandpa Asher,
Uncle Doug & Duane, My Father-in-Law-Tom, Aunt
Therese, Brother-in-law Robert, Godmother Sharon, Budgie,
Papa Joe Budge & Reno, Dick Kernen, Paul Christy,
Aunt Alice & Uncle Cliff, Uncle Earl & Aunt Juanita,
Uncle Cob & Aunt Inie, Aunt Marian & Uncle George,
Big Aunt Inas, Uncle George & Dennis, Billy & Anne H.,
Babe & Geri H., Pat & Lora H., Karl R., Murray,
D.C. & Rochelle, Pat, Ernie and Doug W., Kerry (aka Greg),
Andy D., Robin C., John F., Gary W., Roger M.,
Roger S., Grandma Ruth & Charlie, Pa & Barbara,
Karen & Doc. Groat, Paul B., Uncle Funny, Precious, Wendy,
Bobby & Leona, Bobby C., Little Joe, Torchie, Kay & Jimmy,
Ruby, Roby, Mikey, Danny, Randy, Pudge, Gerry,
Howard, Randy N., Aunt Mabel, O'Shea, Aunt Mary,
Titsi and Louise F., Shirley Schmidt, Father Joe Caroll,
Coach Armstrong, Bonnie Mills, C.S. Keys, Dr. Dale,
Jim S., Bus & Doris, Chuck N., Jane & Dave D., Dave W.,
Jane J., Kim B., The Jacuzzi Queen, Tropical Bob, Max A.,
Lee M., Sammy B., Steve J., Paul P., Bruce W., Eric H.,
Lillian I., Micky F., Ronnie B., Chubby & Mary Mary,
Peggy J., Bob Senn, Jan C., Doyle N., Joe A.,
Joe Cocker and Boo Boo.

CPSIA information can be obtained
at www.ICGtesting.com
Printed in the USA
LVHW090430031121
702322LV00003B/326

9 781737 435600